To You

A little touch of [...] !!

All my love.

Audrey xo.

The man around
the engine

The man around the engine

LIFE BELOW THE WATERLINE

by Vice Admiral Sir Louis Le Bailly

KBE, CB, OBE, DL, C Eng, F Inst Mech E, M I Mar E, F Inst Pet

 KENNETH MASON

Mindful of those who, in the years of war, went
down to the sea in ships and never came back

Published by Kenneth Mason
North Street, Emsworth, Hampshire PO10 7DQ

British Library Cataloguing in Publication Data
Le Bailly, Sir, Louis, 1915-
> *The man around the engine : life below the waterline.*
> *1. Great Britain. Royal Navy. Naval life – Biographies*
> *I. Title*
> *359.1092*

> *ISBN 0-85937-354-1*

Designed and printed in Great Britain

Contents

Illustrations

Preface

Some years ago, Vice-Admiral Sir Ian McGeoch KCB, DSO, DSC, a submariner of renown, urged me to develop the history of how the Royal Navy has reverted to many of the ideas that Admiral Sir John Fisher had introduced forty years before and which the Admiralty abandoned in 1925. A few months later Captain Roskill, the great naval historian, suggested I should put down 'how the navy regained its legs' – ie the mobility that the campaign against Japan showed it had lost. For some time, as so many old men do, I had been scribbling away at my recollections of a rather mixed up career.

These themes generated a hotch-potch of more than 250,000 words and a publisher advised me to split it into two books: one mainly a seagoing autobiography and the other, a largely non-technical history of naval engineers and engineering from 1900 onwards.

The first volume, *The man around the engine*, a phrase taken from Winson Churchill's speech in 1940 to the House of Commons, is part of my own story: under training, at sea and in America in peace and war and peace again; a story that seeks to make three points. First, how the Fisher ideas remained alive within the engineering branch despite reactionary Admiralty decisions in 1925 which helped to cut off the navy from contemporary engineering development and so send it to war technologically backward. Secondly it paints some sort of a picture of what life was like 'down below' during the war for the engineering crews, whose skill, patience, fortitude and courage it was my privilege constantly to observe. Thirdly it concludes with an account of my thirty odd months as Naval Attaché in the United States. Just before I left I was sent a model of a joining shackle – which connects two parts of a warship's cable. This was given as a token of the way the two navies of enormous disparity in size are yet still held together in a storm-proof *Special Relationship*.

The second volume, *From Fisher to the Falklands*, is quite different. The history of how mobility was regained and how officers of all branches including naval and civilian engineers, between the forties and sixties, sometimes with the help of the US navy, contributed to the technological rea-wakening which Fisher had sought (and the Admiralty had once abandoned) is complex. But the result of their efforts is plain. When called on, without notice, in 1982 to fight a sea, land and air campaign for several months on end, 8000 miles from base in the roughest ocean in the world, the navy kept the sea and coped with every kind of emergency and casualty, as it never could have done in 1945. All this is not easy to describe in broad non-technical terms which a lay reader must comprehend. But it should not be impossible. At least I hope not.

My division of the 250,000 words into two parts and the subseqent extensive culling could not have brought forth *The man around the engine* without the help of the editor and the detective work of Jane Jeffree in disentagling the chaos from my word processor. I must acknowledge also the help I have had over the whole project from the Public Records Office, the Imperial War Museum, the Admiralty and RUSI libraries, Group Captain Bolton RAF (retd) the director of the Royal United Services Institute for Defence Studies and many naval engineer officers, the *revolutionaries*, as I have called them, who told me their stories with the same enthusiasm as they had devoted to the improvement of the navy's mobility and thus to its triumph in the Falklands.

I was fortunate to live near the late Vice-Admiral (E) Sir Denys Ford after his retirement and to sup of his wisdom. My debt to the late Vice Admiral Sir Frank Mason for his example and constant encouragement over forty years and his kindness in answering my queries almost till the day of his recent death, can never adequately be expressed. Vice-Admiral Sir George Raper, before his disabling illness took hold, encouraged me and actually drafted some of the script referring to his earlier years in Bath and the problems besetting the technical departments in the twenties and thirties.

Lastly I must thank those officers and officials at the MOD in London and Bath who, over several months, so remorselessly but sympathetically, ploughed through the whole original script and gave it their blessing.

The man around the engine

I wish this afternoon to pay my tribute to the Engineering Branch here in the House of Commons and ask the House to join me so that these many thousands of faithful, skilful, untiring engineers may learn, as they will learn, that we here in London understand what they have done and are doing and that we admire their work and thank them for it. We must never forget the man behind the gun, but we must also remember in these modern times THE MAN AROUND THE ENGINE without whom nothing could be done, who does not see the excitements of the action and does not ask how things are going, but who runs a very big chance of going down with the ship should disaster come.

Winston Churchill, speech in Parliament, February 1940

CHAPTER 1

Dartmouth, 1929-32

See that ye hold fast to the heritage we leave you, yea and teach your children its value that never in the coming centuries their hearts may fail them or their hands grow weak.

(Taken from the College's War Memorial)

AT DINNER ONE EVENING in 1928, after a hard day's skiing in Switzerland, a waiter appeared with a telegram from Gieves, the omniscient naval outfitters, announcing I had passed into the Royal Naval College. Thus ended a family saga to get me to the starting post of my naval career. My father, 25 years a civil engineer in the Middle East and Asia Minor, lost his savings when Turkey entered the war. Then aged 48 and theoretically bankrupt he managed, in quick succession, to return home, to join the Royal Naval Air Service as a recruiting officer and to put my mother in the family way. So it was that I arrived on July 18, 1915 in a tiny flat in Cheyne Court, Chelsea.

In due course my father, fluent in french, was sent to oversee the construction of an airfield at Vendôme and then act as the liaison officer with the local Mairie. There, I have been told, he did much in his humorous way to keep the peace when the frequent crashes and exuberant behaviour of our young naval flyers irritated their French allies. Meanwhile my mother's dormant fundraising ability was stirred so that thanks to a clamour of aunts and great aunts, my brother, ten years my senior, was enabled to go to preparatory school and on to Wellington College, Berkshire whence he won a classical scholarship to Brasenose College, Oxford at the early age of 17.

By early 1919, increasing penury, my father's impending demobilisation and thus the loss of all income drove us under the lee of my widowed maternal grandmother in North Wales. It was she who sent me, under escort, to Llandudno to visit *HMS Lion* then anchored offshore and open to visitors. Prompted no doubt by my mother, she also gave me a picture book, which I still have, entirely devoted to the Royal Navy and entitled *An ABC for Little Britons*. It concluded with some doggerel which would hardly find favour today,

> *Now I am seven I mean to go On the Iron Duke with Jellicoe.*
> *I'll do my best to fire the guns, And sink the warships of the Huns.*
> *When I'm grown up, perhaps I shall Sail as a gold laced Admiral.*
> *I'll wear a sword and cocked hat fine, And never go to bed till nine.*

As a rather unimaginative little boy, but encouraged by my parents who had been told that the navy was a poor man's profession, my future life was thus charted before I was five. A few years later I can still recall my moment of doubt: returning from a visit to my Jersey great aunts in the *SS St Helier* we sailed into storm. Misery enveloped me from the moment we passed the Corbière Lighthouse until we reached Weymouth harbour where, for the first time, I saw *HMS Hood* at close quarters. As the *St Helier* tied up, the *Hood's* brass-funnelled picket boat, driven by a young midshipman seemingly little older than me, dirk at hip, cut through our wash to come smartly alongside the harbour steps. I needed no more and never wavered again.

After a rigorous means test my parents took me one bitter morning to Paddington station. By 1929 even my mother's money-raising efforts were beginning to flag and, although I never knew it for half a century, my reduced fee carried with it my parents' undertaking that if I chose to leave the navy before receiving my commission, they would be charged full fees for my eleven terms at Dartmouth. I was well and truly hooked.

The Drake Term, as we had been told we would be called, came together at the station, eyeing each other's parents for social solecisms, before being handed over to two uniformed cadet captains and the term chief petty officer. Conformity of course was what mattered but my mother, a non-conformist at heart, had seen no reason why she should add to Gieves' bill by buying their standard green trunk when my brother's larger black one remained serviceable. Already hearty station porters, engaged in heaving a green mountain into the luggage van, were making ribald comments about 'one black sheep'. (It was clear too, from the looks of the cadet captains, that all was not what they would have termed shipshape and Bristol fashion.) Speechless with embarrassment, I took a furious farewell of my parents and found a place amongst the others in the carriage.

Four a side we sat, clutching the sandwiches we had been told to bring and gazing shyly at one another while listening to the well meant but wholly uncomprehended words of advice from our mentors. As we neared the River Dart the navy seemed the more frightening and our chosen careers correspondingly less attractive. At the Kingswear terminus we huddled aboard *The Mew*, to be ferried across with our 41 green and one large black trunk to the Dartmouth pontoon. In our new caps, far too large, and British Warm overcoats, we were 'marched' although that word hardly describes our graceless progress through the rain-driven streets to the College of which, for so long, we had dreamed.

Most of us were reasonably intelligent and, often, quite athletic children. Academically we were towards the top of the Common Entrance standard. I had only just failed a scholarship to Wellington (a standby in case I failed Dartmouth) and there were several up to Winchester level. For each of us who had boarded the train at Paddington, five or six, by a mysterious interview process, which would have reduced today's psychologists

• *Four years at Dartmouth prepared Cadet Le Bailly for a career he was not to follow*

to tears, had been turned down.   We were not aware of it, we certainly didn't feel like it, but by some quirky yardstick we could have been dubbed an élite.

At Dartmouth we lived under the dominion of the past.   On our first night, as we lay 'at attention' in our beds, shivering to the chill January winds blowing through the open windows, the cadet gunner, a fearsome warrant oficer of imposing mien, paraded slowly down the dormitory, rather like the beadle in *Oliver Twist*. Above his head he held a cane thicker than anything we had known at our preparatory schools.   He commanded us to look carefully at what, without doubt, all would soon feel.

The pedagogues of the Dartmouth academic establishment, bachelors almost to a man, linked us to the wooden walls of the old *Britannia*; and soaked us in its traditions.   They were abetted by uniformed Term Officers of the executive category who had been their pupils shortly before.   For most naval officers, the thirties was a period when the odds against promotion to commander were at least three or four to one but an appointment to the College as a term officer shortened these odds and success could well tip the balance.   Thus the performance of his term at games, in sailing and pulling (rowing) boats, as well as on the parade ground (but never as far as I can establish in the class room), could give a quite dramatic push up the greasy promotion pole to the term officer concerned.

Unhappily for the cadets of that era, there was acute sexual frustration among married term officers due to a College rule that forbade them housing a wife nearer than Plymouth, 30 miles away.   Thus there was no soothing balm readily available to tone down the irritations emanating from the 40 or so near adolescents who were the term officer's particular responsibility.

With hindsight I think we were led to believe that the engineer officers on the Dartmouth staff were cast in a mould different from their executive counterparts, that the (E) officers, training at the Royal Naval Engineering College at Keyham were a crowd of beer-swilling, rugger-playing louts who came mostly from public schools and who were therefore damned from the start, or from the artificer's training establishment, and therefore to be looked down on as 'cuckoos in the nest'.   It took time for us to realise, partly from listening to the engineer-commander (specially selected from the Royal Yacht) or his (E) subordinates, when they lectured us, or when we met them off duty that, on the whole, they were as talented as their executive colleagues, more individual and more relaxed.

The gap between executives and engineers was only part of the divisive Dartmouth tradition: there was also a schism between naval officers and academics. Whilst the latter permitted the former to enter their common room for morning coffee, it was a rare privilege for any master to be invited into the wardroom and almost unique for a civilian to become a member of the mess and so drink and feed with the uniformed 'élite'. A similar divisiveness was enforced on the cadets. None could address another in a term senior to his, it was equally heinous for a senior cadet to speak to a junior, except on saturday evenings within certain well patrolled and closely defined areas. But on dance nights when the cadet dance band played on the quarterdeck (main assembly hall) cadets were permitted to dance with each other, although not too often with the same partner. For those brave enough, there were three well developed College nursing sisters whose duty it seemed included introducing older cadets to the pleasures of holding the female form in not too restrictive an embrace.

For Drake Term Dartmouth quickly settled into routine. The first ring of the firebell at six am sent us naked down the dormitory through an icy, over-chlorinated plunge bath and out again before the ringing stopped. Betowelled but still wet we stood at attention in front of our basins awaiting the order *wash necks*, followed by *wash teeth*. As 0610 approached, the order came to *get dressed* followed five minutes later by *say prayers*. After early morning studies life was conducted at the double. We doubled to breakfast and rushed it so that we could get a chance to secure a cubicle containing rough square pieces of paper known as 'admiralty brown'. Then to the parade ground for divisions, from where we doubled to our classroom or down several hundred steps to the river for engineering or sailing instruction. In the afternoon we played a team game, ran several miles, sailed, swam, played squash, shot on the range or went beagling. Each type of activity was defined as a 'log' or 'half a log'; and a full log had to be completed each day and entered in a book which was inspected by the cadet captain. Eventually we changed, doubled away to evening classes, to supper and so to bed.

Any slackness or breach, 'Guff', was punished with the cane by the cadet captain. For more serious crimes such as smoking or drinking there was punishment known as Official Cuts or more colloquially as OC. Somewhere between the beatings for Guff and Official Cuts, lay punishments known as Strafes, awarded for such incomprehensible crimes as lack of term spirit, slackness on parade, or just plain slackness, conducted personally by the term officer, assisted by the two term cadet captains. Each of the three of course was armed with a cane to inflict the conventional, but always painful, penalty on those who were last, had a button out of place, shoe-lace undone or who exceeded the time limit for whatever evolution was in progress. Poor or rich, bright or dim, Dartmouth took and hammered us as hard as it legally could, and perhaps harder, into what it hoped would be a single pattern.

Some could not stand it and induced their parents to remove them, whatever the cost. A few overcame the system and retained their individuality more or less unscarred. I was not one of those but was fortunate that one such became my closest friend. Born of a long naval line he had a joyous contempt for the whole regime. Doing his level best to avoid team games because they bored him, he ate well at the canteen run by Chief Petty Officer ('Daddy') Lavers and his daughters (known as The Hags) because he could afford the good things of life. Neither popular nor unpopular he would not have cared a jot either way. He did the minimum work to pass the termly exams; that mysterious thing about which we were so often lectured, the term spirit, left him wholly unmoved.

But it was he who sustained me with his mordant humour as he was to sustain so many others in the bloody years ahead. The same equable spirit took him, on a precious leave from his ship, into a Hampden bomber over Germany when he heard the RAF were short of navigators. Then he found himself in command of a fireship destined for a one-way trip to Calais or Boulogne. Further service in motor torpedo boats and then in an old river gunboat, finally sunk off the North African coast, failed to satisfy his thirst for action. He failed also to satisfy the authorities because he inadvertently left behind a few Confidential Books of no great security classification when he was at last picked out of a Carley float, after many hours in the blazing sun, holding a young dying sailor in his arms. Reappointed, as he was told for this *serious security lapse*, to a cruiser whose senior officers he quickly came to regard as not only pompous but craven, he went to the cable office in Alexandria and sent a telegram of such defamatory frankness to his elder brother, then naval assistant to the first sea lord, that the censors in Egypt stopped it and reported him. As a result he was immediately appointed to an exceptionally dangerous job at Tobruk then under siege. Rather than take a lengthy passage in a hospital ship, as instructed, which might have been reasonably safe, he preferred to stay a little longer in Alexandria to procure sufficient khaki uniform and use his friends in the RAF to fly him to Tobruk. When the plane crashed on take-off, killing the pilot and bursting into flames, he returned rather singed to the Cecil Hotel in Alexandria, and ordered up some new uniforms.

It was then, I think, he began to believe his luck was running out, for whom should he spot in the next room but Admiral Cunningham's new chief of staff who had probably saved him from a court martial for his telegram but who was certainly under the illusion that this brave and tempestuous spirit was now immured in besieged Tobruk. Anyway, on returning from a dash to Malta in the cruiser in which I was serving, I received a note indicating the number of his room at the Cecil and asking me to bring a pair of dark glasses. Together, we crept past the adjoining room and went for what I think we both knew might well be a last blow out. After dinner, hearing how difficult I found it to stay awake and alert for the five-day run to Malta and back, he did me one last service and took me to a chemist who sold us both 500 Benzedrine tablets.

My ship battled its way to Malta and back the following week and on our return I read the casualty list resulting from the loss of *HMAS Parramatta*. So, in the company of many brave Australians, with whom he always felt at home, Dick Litchfield paid the price of admiralty as I believe he always knew he would. He proved much in his too short life: that the Dartmouth system was not omnipotent and that the unique qualities which the College seemed to esteem were certainly not detrimental to the navy if they appeared missing, as they certainly were in his case. Tradition, I have always believed, is something to be lived up to. Dartmouth, in the early thirties clung to the idea that tradition was something to be lived on. It is said that the man of character in peace is generally the man of courage in war: Dick Litchfield proved that correct. But the assessment of character is an imprecise business and to be approached with caution. In the thirties, the Royal Navy had yet to learn that lesson: let us hope it has now.

For the majority of us who feared to buck it or were cast in a malleable mould, few ordeals in war were as bad as our time at Dartmouth. And a true tale suggests that my judgement is shared by others. After six years of continuous war as sea, when a few dozen ships from the Royal and Commonwealth Navies were anchored in Tokyo Bay at the time of the Japan's surrender, there were many accounts of the brutalities inflicted on allied prisoners of war. Only one I heard had a grain of humour. The man, a lieutenant-commander, who in later years was to become a famous British admiral and then Gentleman Usher of the Black Rod, had found himself senior officer of a POW camp. It was generally agreed that it was largely his enduring fortitude and courage which had sustained his fellow prisoners.

How did you stand it? one of the doctors asked when he saw the wounds.

Well, four years at Dartmouth helped, was the cheerful reply from the small, scarred and emaciated figure.

Somehow, in the Dartmouth process, we managed to build a veneer of manhood before our time. Statistically, Lord Moran seems to suggest, fewer of those with a Dartmouth upbringing broke under the strain of modern war at sea than those with a more conventional education. Painful though it had certainly been, perhaps, in the end, that is what it was all about.

CHAPTER 2

HMS Hood, 1932-33

*Long before the Hitler Youth was thought of, the Navy caught him young
and soaked him in the pride and joy of a great tradition.*
The Anatomy of Courage Lord Moran, Constable

LOOKING BACK ON the autumn of 1931 it is now quite baffling
how little about the Invergordon mutiny trickled down to the
cadets. Perhaps our term officers knew little themselves or felt
that the blazing ineptitude of the Admiralty and the breach of faith
with those sailors on the 1919 pay code should not be passed to
young and immature officers. A more imaginative approach
would have drawn some lessons from which junior officers, soon
to join the fleet, might have profited.

Jutland, the near starvation of Britain by German submarines
and the east coast's bombardment by the German fleet had
diminished national pride in the navy. When the truth of
Invergordon became known, it nearly destroyed public faith
altogether; and it helped to knock Britain off the gold standard in
September 1931. These wartime German naval successes had
already produced another reaction. A series of backward looking
Boards of Admiralty, anxious to discard responsibility for such
evident failures, had decided by 1925 to revert as far as possible to
pre-Fisher traditions. Promotion from the lower deck was to be
discouraged, old type engineers and the more troublesome (E)
officers were to be relegated to a non-executive (virtually civilian)
status from which Fisher had rescued them. Whilst paradoxi-
cally, by the thirties, staff training, introduced by Sir Eric Geddes
and Beatty, after years of resistance by Fisher, was still mistrusted

as inimical to good personal leadership and therefore an added cause of the Invergordon affair.

These failures, some real, some imaginary, together with the recent incidents of indiscipline, culminating in the full-scale mutiny at Invergordon, quite suddenly coalesced. The result was a powerful advocacy led by the first lord himself, Sir Bolton Eyres-Monsell, who had gone to sea as a midshipman in 1896, for a reintroduction of sail training, an idea instantly seized on by press and public as a panacea for the navy's ills. Fisher's 'machinery' education and Battenberg's 'democracy' could now finally be eliminated. Cadets and boy bluejackets, all in white duck bell-bottoms, holystoning the decks and swarming aloft onto the yardarms, that surely was the answer.

Happily one result of Invergordon was a new Board of Admiralty and a new commander in chief of the Atlantic Fleet. Best of all, Admiral Sir Ernle Chatfield, then C-in-C Mediterranean Fleet, became First Sea Lord and matters started to improve. Admiral Sir John D Kelly (brought back onto the active list on the advice of King George V) restored discipline to the now renamed Home Fleet. The first lord's pressure to resume sail training was successfully resisted, albeit by a compromise: a training cruiser was commissioned, to which all cadets leaving Dartmouth, and those joining the navy through the Public Schools (Special Entry system), would be appointed.

So Drake Term became the last to leave Dartmouth and go directly to the fleet as cadets. Thus it was that Dick Litchfield, I and two others, foregathered at the Keppel's Head, Portsmouth, one evening in early August 1932. From our modest attic bedrooms we could see the quarterdeck of the great ship which was to be our home. Next morning, clad in our number one uniforms, we duly repaired on board. Although like most of my generation I had read Charles Morgan's *The Gunroom* and was well prepared, by four years at Dartmouth, for the sadistic bullying of junior midshipmen which Morgan so vividly portrayed, the reality in *HMS Hood* (and I believe in the rest of the fleet) was wholly different. From the moment we reported to the officer of the watch, the whole rhythm of life was a boy's dream come true. They were all there, as Taffrail and Bartimeus had told us they would be: Guns and Torps, the Springer and the Pilot, the Schoolie and the Chief and the Senior, the Chippie, the Bo'sun, the PMO and of course our lord and master the Sub. Best of all were the brass-funnelled picket boats. On these we spent on Brasso what was left of our three shillings and sixpence daily pay after we had settled our mess bills!

From 0600, when we slipped out of our hammocks for PT, arms drill or polishing the huge brass stove at the sub-lieutenant's end of the gunroom, until ten in the evening we rarely stopped or wanted to. Always we were learning. We learned to be alert night and day for the pipe and shrill cry of *Awaaaay picket boat's crew*, when we would race for the great lower boom projecting from the ship's side aft of the fx'le but a few inches wide and 20 feet above the boat tossing below. We learned to run along it and to slide down the jackstay with only 10 minutes to bring the boat to the gangway. We learned, too, the knack of driving a picket boat through half a gale when full of cheerful senior officers returning late at night and in no mood to accept a wave in the sternsheets. We learned to take a launch, full of tipsy and retching libertymen, through a rough sea and how best to still their songs or fights beyond earshot of the ship. We learned how to take sunsights at noon and starsights at dawn and dusk, to keep watch on the hundred-yard quarterdeck in harbour and to run the routine

• *Author, extreme right, recording practice sun sights in spring 1933. Next to him is Midshipman, later Vice Admiral Sir Charles, Mills*

which governed the lives of 1500 men, for ever keeping an eye on the weather and the rest of the fleet.

At sea we learned how to turn the great slabs of gritty chocolate into drinkable cocoa and take it, unspilled, to the officer of the watch. We learned how to stand on the bridge for hours on end peering into the night through rain, sleet and snow or, in fog, on the open wings of the bridge keeping in sight the fog buoy trailed by our next ahead. There was bookwork too: the theory of gunnery, torpedoes, wireless, navigation and engineering drummed into us by patient petty officers and our instructor lieutenant-commander. By some miracle and because it fascinated me, I had won the Navigation Prize at Dartmouth, so the job of tanky (navigator's assistant) later fell to my lot. This coveted post required my presence by day or night when either of my particular deities the navigator or his assistant lieutenant (N) were on the bridge or decided that the ship's course or speed needed alteration. I found myself a secret caboose in the bridge structure where I could curl up at night. There the midshipman of the watch could quickly find me if my masters appeared. And the chronometers, on which accurate navigation depended, were my responsibility to wind each week.

Above all we learned about sailors: from our hammock boys, who lashed up or unlashed our hammocks each morning and evening, the only people on board younger and financially poorer than we were (despite the small subvention we gave them); from our boats' crews, from the lordly chief and petty officers, from the cooper, still plying his trade, from that now unhappily extinct dinosaur, the Royal Marine gunner and from his fellow warrant officers; from them all more than any formal lecture or book could teach us. We came to understand, as we went about our business on the messdecks, that there were worse meals than our Maltese messman produced. We learned, too, that a married sailor could just about keep his family above the poverty line if he never went ashore, if he added to his pay by taking in an officer's washing, cutting hair or working in a PO's mess as messman (waiter) or by making beautiful rope grommets for our telescopes.

We even savoured the world of the chief and petty officers. Separated from the messdecks by a waist-high partition and some dusty curtains, they could have neat rum each day instead of grog (rum and water), they carried immense responsibility and could look forward to a small pension after 22 years of faithful service and family separation. For a few chief petty officers there was the big jump to the warrant officer's mess. Here were the barons, men of vast experience who knew all there was to know about sailors, who lived a very private life off duty in a mess into which few wardroom officers penetrated. Infinitely kind to midshipmen, but set in their ways, they were rightly regarded with awe by junior lieutenants.

There was little time for recreation. At sea we played deck hockey on the quarterdeck, an exhausting and often bloody game with a rope grommet puck, bent walking sticks and no rules. In harbour we played hockey, soccer or, if brave enough, rugger with the sailors and, when the fleet was at Rosyth, long cross-country races for the Arbuthnot Trophy. If given leave, which was rare, it always expired with the officer's boat at 1915 just giving us time to change into uniform for our evening meal. Dinner, as with our other meals, was dispensed by the same wily Maltese messman and his acolytes who took a shilling a day from our pay. Our winebill was limited to 10 shillings a month as cadets and 15 shillings as midshipmen. On this we could treat ourselves to a sherry, a glass of beer on guest nights and an occasional glass of Marsala when we returned, cold and shivering, with our boat cloaks and uniforms wet through from a rough boat trip. Spirits, had we been allowed them, were almost unknown to us and few could afford or wished to smoke.

Even after half a century incidents from that happy year come to mind. At the end of the autumn cruise when *Hood* dropped anchor at Spithead with the wind and tide astern the cable holder brake failed to operate effectively. The huge cable could run out and part. The first lieutenant (a gunnery officer) used all his magnificent vocal powers to clear the fx'le. Then we retreated to the eyes of the ship where, he comfortingly told me, we should *probably* be safe. Fortunately the cable holder brake began to hold with less than half a cable of chain left in the locker. Two months later, with the whole Home Fleet anchored in Vigo Bay, there was a night attack exercise by the fleet picket boats simulating motor torpedo boats. My picket boat led a feint attack and was soon spotted and held by a dozen searchlights as the real attack came in successfully from the other side. The result was an appalling attack of 'searchlight eye' which sent me into the sickbay. Twenty-four hours later I was well enough for leave in Villagarcia where I played roulette for the first time and, for the only time in my life,

•*How to get searchlight eye. Attack by picket boats*

won.   On the way to Gibraltar someone decided to establish
whether the recently fitted anti-aircraft guns abreast the main-
mast could be operated with 'X' turret's 15 in guns fired full
charge on a forward bearing.   Inevitably a midshipman's gun's
crew became the guinea pigs.   The six of us selected were nearly
blown overboard and the three of us who survived the war are all
deaf!

Gibraltar was a halcyon period: hockey, played on a dust
pitch with anti-tetanus injections for scraped knees; ginger beer
and chocolate biscuits at the club after the games; races with the
sailors up the Rock to inspect the apes; a route march through the
town; a concert party in the coal shed.   Later I found myself in
charge of a 12-oared cutter taking the retiring Governor of Gibraltar ashore from the flagship.   From Gibraltar we moved to Algiers
where one of my near contemporaries doing his destroyer time
ran away and joined the Foreign Legion.   Brought back after some
weeks of diplomatic activity and the recipient of Their Lordship's
displeasure he and I next met when, as a rear-admiral, he became
my instructor at the Imperial Defence College.

I ran my beloved picket boat for the whole of that spring cruise until relieved of my duty and that of tanky to become one of two midshipmen charged with the running of *Hood's* singularly unmanoeuverable drifter, *HMD Horizon*. Coal-fired, her boilers served steam reciprocating engines driving a single large propeller. In those days, as a relic of the first war, each battleship or battlecruiser had attached to her one such drifter as a maid of all work. A couple of hundred libertymen, several tons of potatoes or cabbages, firebricks, drums of lubricating oil, everything large in numbers or dirty came our way. But there was (to me) a very grand bridge, all of eight by six feet, the wheelhouse directly below, and a crew of 12. The wardroom, constructed in the fishhold, could conveniently accommodate four for meals and three for sleep: one body on each bench beside the table and the third on it. The ship's company lived in even greater discomfort. On passage, for which we embarked the sub or a junior lieutenant as acting captain when we sailed ahead of the fleet, we received hard lying money, as welcome to the midshipmen as to sailors and stokers. But in harbour, for 24 hours out of 48, she was my sole responsibility. Stormy nights in the Firth of Forth, Cromarty or Scapa, with gusting winds and sometimes a strong tide, called for judgement and sea sense with little margin for error. Many were the trials and tribulations of the coxswain and engine room crew as a 17-year old learned the tricks. Happily summer nights were short in the north and drifters, like warships, were strongly built. Somehow we survived.

By the summer of 1933, 20 months or so after Invergordon, the unfair pay cuts had been ironed out and the trouble makers discharged. Admiral Sir John Kelly, the C-in-C, and our own ACQ (admiral commanding battle cruisers) Rear-Admiral (later Admiral Sir William) James (Bubbles) had impressed their personalities on the fleet. Captain Binney (afterwards Admiral Sir Thomas Binney and Governor of Tasmania) who had joined *Hood* on nearly the same day as we had (and who had been on our selection board when we entered Dartmouth) had similarly impressed the ship's company. Admiral James and Captain Binney, with Commander McCrum, the latter immensely popular with the sailors, and his faithful ally Lieutenant-Commander Harry Pursey, one of the few lower deck officers to have reached the wardroom (later an MP of note), set out to imbue the ship's company with the idea that the *Hood* should win the forthcoming fleet regatta. The gunroom soon discovered that we had a vital part to play in this. Traditionally the fleet gunrooms raced gigs for the Battenberg Trophy the day before the main regatta. A win by *Hood's* gunroom would be taken as a good augury for the following day. Failure however would be regarded as a bad omen against the ship becoming Cock of the Fleet.

Then short and lean I was, I suppose, the obvious choice for coxswain. But for those who were to undertake the hard work we gathered a formidable crew; Beckwith as stroke, Thurstan, Wainwright, Charles, MacFarlane and Gray. Sadly only three of the seven were to survive the war. But we were young and enthusiastic and how we trained. The chaplain, the Rev J C Waters, himself a notable oarsman was in charge and the new sub, Aylwin, urbane and highly civilised, also took a hand. Even the messman's food improved (subsidised by the wardroom I heard many years later). We practised at dawn and dusk and some afternoons too. I found my duties included taking charge of the methylated spirit for blistered hands and bottoms. Gig's thwarts, however well polished, were not far removed from sandpaper. We trained so hard that one day in the Cromarty Firth, the chaplain gave us an afternoon off to play the wardroom at golf on the lovely course at Nigg, (alas no longer in use). Later we were also to be the wardroom's guests in the pub (still there). Thus it was, at peace with ourselves, and pleasantly tipsy from a modest, but, for us, unusual quantity of McEwans Scotch Ale, that we walked back to the jetty through the heather-scented twilight to the sorrowful questing note of a curlew. I remember shivering, as if drenched in ice, and putting it down to the McEwans I had imbibed. But it was late in May, possibly the 24th, the day *HMS Hood* blew up in 1941 in action with the *Bismark* and all but three of her 1500 crew lost.

Hood's gunroom won the Battenberg Trophy: and next day we raced again and won again. Much money changed hands as *Hood* became Cock of the Fleet. That evening Captain Binney sent down a case of champagne to the gunroom. Later I have a faint recollection of an invading posse of midshipmen from one of the battleships carrying me forcibly to our wardroom and casting me through the door, when I knew no more. The next morning I awoke with the first of a lifetime of hangovers, recovering sufficiently to go over with the rest of the crews to *HMS Nelson* to receive our trophies from the great John Kelly himself.

• *Our cups*
floweth over

Either as a mark of favour or because I looked as though I needed fresh air, I learned I was to sail that evening for Portsmouth as *Horizon's* navigator and one of the two watchkeepers under a young lieutenant, a trip of challenge. Although we midshipmen had run *Horizon* in harbour neither of us had watchkeeping certificates and had never kept watch alone in open waters. There was more to it than that. In theory *Horizon* carried enough coal for the voyage but some years before a similar fleet drifter, *Blue Sky*, on precisely the same trip had been lost with all hands in circumstances never explained. For this reason we were instructed to close certain shore wireless stations down the east coast and report our position by morse radio. We reached Portsmouth with, literally, only a few shovelfulls of coal left in our bunkers. This trivial saga was a milestone for me, signalling the end of a seaman's career and the start of another which, initially I viewed with distaste. For before leaving Dartmouth one of my eyes had shown signs of falling below the hawkish vision needed in those pre-radar days. A further test confirmed this. If I stayed at sea and there was no improvement by the time I came to receive my commission, I was told I should be out on my ear. If I left the navy at once I would be excused Responsions at Oxford; if I joined the army I could go either to Woolwich or Sandhurst; if I stayed in the navy it would have to be as paymaster or engineer.

Oxford was out financially and I could face neither the army nor a paymaster's job. That left two options: hope for the best and risk finding myself unemployed and lacking qualifications at the age of 20, or specialise in engineering. A former term officer at

Dartmouth dined me in the royal yacht (where he was senior engineer) and persuaded me that engineering it should be. *Hood's* Captain Binney told me, *Engineers have to place in the hands of those who fight the naval battle the most effective weapons that the state of the art can achieve; and then go into battle with those weapons and keep them operational as long as they are needed.* When he saw that my doubts still lingered he added, *Mobility is by no means the least though perhaps the oldest of these weapons. Do you not think it is worth staying in the navy that I know you love, to sharpen and help wield it?*

Few midshipmen have had wiser counsel.

The wheels started to turn but first I had a short reprieve. *Hood's* gunroom were detailed to man *HMS Victory II*, a replica of Nelson's flagship built on the hull of a 50ft launch. In appropriate dress we sailed between Margate and Swanage advertising Navy Week at various resorts. Apart from Bournemouth where the press headlined, *Midshipmen with their Midshipmaids*, which evoked an excessively stuffy signal from the Admiralty, we emerged both virginal and unscathed. Eventually I had to discard my dirk and telescope, sew purple stripes on my sleeves and officially become a 'civilian' in the Royal Navy. After a couple of weeks' leave I traded in my rather worn out Morris Cowley (cost £5) for a Swift (£10) with a gate gear, an outside handbrake and a dickey seat. Full of foreboding I proceeded westwards at a steady 25mph to the Royal Naval Engineering College at Keyham, near Devonport.

•*HMS Hood at Cromarty Forth, 1933*

CHAPTER 3

Keyham, 1933-1937

The gentleman with the little velvet slip between the gold rings on his sleeve does his unnoticed work. If anything goes wrong, if he overlooks a subordinate's error, he will not be wigged by the Admiral in god's open air. He will be peeled, flayed, blinded or boiled. That is his hourly risk ... 'An they come into the wardroom,' says Twenty One, 'and you know they've been having a young hell of a time down below, but they never growl at us or get stuffy or anything. No end good men I swear they are.'
A Fleet in Being Rudyard Kipling

THE ROYAL NAVAL Engineering College (generally known as Keyham) had particularly unsalubrious surroundings. If the wind blew from the west, as it usually did, we lived in the effluent of the dockyard foundry; if it came from the east then the adjacent Devonport gasworks' smell was our constant companion. There were about 100 officers under instruction, 'students' as they were generally known, which number included a contingent from the old Dominions and occasionally China. Midshipmen and sub-lieutenants had cubicles. Leave for midshipmen, permitted only on two evenings a week if formally applied for, ended at 7.15 pm. Most of the officers under instruction were the same public schoolboys I had been taught to despise. A few, like me, were 'second choice' engineers. In their case, however, this was often due to poor marks in the entry examination which made their going hard. I viewed the whole set up with a deep loathing but by the end of my four years' incarceration I had come to love it.

Over the years I have learned that naval engineers need to bridge the gap between the best of industry's current technology and the likely trends foreshadowed by research on the one hand and operational requirements, always within limited time and money, on the other. To accomplish this the naval engineer has to be sufficiently broad-minded and professionally skilled to achieve both the respect and understanding of scientists dreaming into the future and of the naval staff concerned mainly with threats, present and presumed. The naval engineer must also judge what 'the market' can stand in terms of climate, rough salt sea, the navy's human material and the military and economic fighting potential, as far as intelligence can define it, of likely enemies. It is a heavy responsibility which the early professional training, on which I embarked so distrustfully, provided only the first lesson.

In the late twenties and thirties naval officer entry to a diminished navy was severely restricted. Public schoolmasters and parents, mindful of the post-world war one Geddes Axe, forebore to 'push' the navy. In preparatory schools however a Dartmouth cadetship was still a valuable addition to the honours board and therefore a career to be promoted. Initially there was always slight antagonism between the comparatively few and much younger, though fleet-experienced, Darts and the more numerous Pubs. There were several ways in which Keyham achieved their amalgamation. First there was the instruction in theoretical and practical work which at Dartmouth we had been taught to accept and not question. The Pub was more inclined to think and doubt which rubbed off on the Darts. In practical dockyard work, however, time already spent by the Darts in chipping, filing, pattern-making, moulding, casting and use of a lathe gave them an early edge on the rest.

That a common spirit emerged was due to the calibre of the instructional staff, carefully selected (E) officers many of whom were to rise to the top. Among the more senior were several trained under the pre-world war one Selborne-Fisher scheme which had abolished the old type engineer and had elevated the new type (E) specialist to the status enjoyed by gunnery, navigation and torpedo executive officers. Fisher had wished them to be interchangeable and several staff members held bridge as well as engine-room watchkeeping certificates. Unhappily a reactionary Admiralty, worried at the navy's poor showing in world war one, lumped the blame on Fisher and abolished the whole arrangement a few years before I became an unwilling (E) specialist. Once again engineers had been relegated in the naval pecking order. Like the staff (E) specialists the naval instructor officers and civilians were handpicked, competent teachers and personalities in their own right. Although instructors wore a lieutenant-commander's or commander's stripes and, like engineers, were low in the pecking order, all had fought through the first world war in one or other of the services. Several were much decorated and some had achieved high temporary rank which gave them confidence and authority in their dealings with the young.

Specialists, instructors and civilians dined formally with the students once a week so that our learning was not confined to classroom. They became friends and enlarged our horizons. Our captain-in-charge (with no disciplinary powers over us or the few stokers attached to the College) was an old type engineer who had won a DSO at Zeebrugge. He, his wife and young family, by modest parties in their home and picnics on Dartmoor, played a considerable part in the civilising process as did our stewards and the remarkable crew of workshop instructors. All were ex-service men of the highest calibre, all determined that we should live up to their standards. In this closed community existed a quite extraordinary spirit which even unwilling newcomers could not but recognise. It was on the games field that this spirit shone. Few people today with knowledge of west country rugby football would credit that from 100 young officers and a dozen youngish staff officers it was possible to field two good hockey sides including navy and England caps and three rugby fifteens. Besides providing players for Devonport Services and the navy as a matter of course (sometimes for England, Wales and Ireland too) the first fifteen competed on equal terms with Plymouth Albion, Redruth, Camborne, Penzance and touring Oxford and Cambridge sides as well.

To confine vigorous young men in a classroom until 4.15 on four days a week left little time for recreational training, especially in the winter. But the custom, more compelling than any rule, was that all should go down to the playing field to train under two great coaches, an ex master-at-arms and an ex-Royal Marine, both with navy and England caps. And train we did till after dark. A day or two missed incurred no comment but following a prolonged lapse the eventual return to the field could be a singularly exhausting experience! Stan Kealey and Ernie Gardiner were the best of friends to us but the hardest of masters. I doubt if any single RN group was as fit as the Keyham officers in those days.

This tradition of excellence on the playing field, despite the scorn of the elderly Dartmouth academics, was essential to our overall training. In the early days of steam, perils below were real and frightening with which only those possessing engineering qualifications could cope. At Dartmouth we had stoked the coal boilers of our attendant sloop *HMS Forres* – coal was in use in many ships but the change to oil-fired installations opened the way to higher pressures and steam temperatures. Lagging techniques and heat removal had not kept pace nor had jointing techniques, so steam leaks were frequent. Heat and humidity below, always bad, had worsened so that heat stroke and exhaustion were common. To lead in such conditions required superlative fitness. Thus was it regarded as essential for (E) officers.

An élite vitalises its parent institution by enhancing its dynamism. Such was the Quart Club. Initiated by Sub-Lieutenants King-Lewis and Wilkinson soon after the Admiralty abrogation of the Fisher scheme, the Great Betrayal, it serves today's new Royal Naval Engineering College at Manadon, outside Plymouth as it served Keyham. When, after 50 years as president, (by now) Dr King Lewis retired from that post, I was proud to succeed him. In turn I handed over the presidency to an (E) officer I had taught when he was a midshipman, now Admiral Sir William Pillar GBE. After serving on the Board of Admiralty and as Commandant of the Royal College of Defence Studies he is a member of the Royal Yacht Squadron and Lieutenant-Governor of Jersey. The (E) branch has come a long way in the last 40 years.

The two most telling influences at Keyham arrived towards the end of my midshipman's time. The Dean of the College, then a commander (E) responsible for all instruction, had served in the same post three years or so before. I have his notes of his farewell speech at the end of his first incumbency which show the way his mind was moving.

We need a collective superiority complex based on the realisation that we are putting up an increasingly good performance. Whale Island (HMS Excellent, the Gunnery School) and Vernon (Torpedo School) have gone about telling everybody that they are the salt of the earth and the astonishing thing is that a great number of people have begun to believe them. Now if there is one branch of the service more than another which can lay claim to this savouring quality, it is the engineering branch.

When you look back on the war you will see that the guns hit - fairly frequently; that the torpedoes kept their depth - sometimes; and the mines - well you all know the remark passed by a submarine engine room artificer as something went bump, bump, bump down the side - 'Good old Vernon. Another dud'.

But engine room machinery ALWAYS developed full power, and sometimes, when required, a bit more. This achievement was obtained not by us who are the products of the new (E) scheme but by those of the old scheme and we ought to take off our hats to them. But having established a right - as a branch - to a superiority complex, what are we going to do about it? We must know our job thoroughly, not superficially. We must be able to give a detailed answer, in comprehensible language, to a technical question and see to it that our shares are on a rising market, not only technically but socially. We want golden opinions in other activities besides football. We need big ideas if Keyham is to be the hub of the engineering branch as Whale Island and Vernon are the centres of their activities.

Commander, later Rear Admiral, (E) Charles Pierre Berthon had joined in the early days of the Selborne-Fisher scheme. After obtaining his bridge watchkeeping certificate, thus qualifying him as an executive officer, and an engine room watchkeeping certificate, he became chief engineer of a steam-driven K-Class fleet submarine where he temporarily succeeded to command, as Fisher would have wished, when his captain fell sick. The Great Betrayal was something Berthon set himself with charm and strength of purpose to reverse by starting with the 100 young (E) officers for whose training, again, he found himself responsible on this his second appointment as Dean. Happily I was one of them.

Living close by he often dined in, guest night or not, and frequently visited the two ante-rooms, drinking beer with the midshipmen or gimlets (gin and lime, the 'in' drink of those days) with the sub-lieutenants. His message, delivered in a dozen different ways was invariable.

(E) officers had to win the trust and affection of their executive counterparts not by reacting to slights and ill-mannered snobbishness, but by showing that they could equal or, where possible, excel executive officers in every field. Technology was the foundation upon which the

•*Rear-Admiral Peter Berthon whom the author came to know as father-in-law*

navy's future would be built, but to be a good technologist was not enough. Anyone who shirked his theoretical or practical work would soon be out on his ear, but he who worked hard and successfully would be allowed whatever time off was needed to play hard. Many executive officers hunted and the Dartmoor was in need of a bigger field. What were we waiting for? Executive officers played polo in Malta and elsewhere; so must (E) officers. Executive officers found time to shoot; Keyham must have a shoot. Executive officers often fished; why had Keyham not got a beat on the nearby Dart or Tamar? Mountaineering, sailing, skiing, rock-climbing, there were surely many other activities besides rugby. Executive officers broadened their Dartmouth-confined lives during their sub-lieutenants courses at Greenwich and Portsmouth; somehow the same must be contrived in the less sophisticated south-west.

Such ideas would cost money and Keyham was poor. By virtue of his seniority Berthon was also mess president, so the messman, into whose pockets so much of our money went, was sacked and the mess turned into a self-financing organisation with a salaried mess caterer. The results were electrifying and sports subsidies quickly became available. Nor did Berthon stop there. As the College's senior Selborne-Fisher scheme officer he wrote officially, through the like-minded engineer captain in charge, to the engineer-in-chief. In fairly strong language he expressed the view that the College was far too small for the number of (E) officers needed by the rearmament programme, was ill-equipped and should be moved lock, stock and barrel to the Portsmouth area where it would be nearer London and the other executive specialist schools. This was not at all well received. The engineer-in-chief responded stuffily and although agreeing that the planned number of students would be too large for Keyham to handle, insisted that *close proximity to a dockyard for instruction in practical work was essential. The college would therefore stay in the Plymouth area. Further he was negotiating for the use of Raglan Barracks close to the dockyard.*

Undeterred by this broadside and the loss of the Portsmouth battle, Berthon induced the Admiralty to buy the Hall-Parlby estate at Manadon, although London's procrastination resulted in achieving only two thirds of the estate for the original asking price of the whole. Today on that site, unarguably, stands the greatest naval engineering college in the world, a fitting monument to Berthon's imaginative foresight and courageous persistence.

But even that was not all Berthon did for the (E) branch during his second spell as dean. By pressuring the chaplain of the fleet he gave us Reggie, the Reverend R R Churchill. Reckless Reggie as he was known throughout the navy was the most remarkable personality thrown up by that notoriously eccentric and lovable crew of clerics, the naval chaplains. Reggie's benign influence as friend and confidante of the sailors at Invergordon most surely helped to cool their justifiable discontent. And his long-term friendship with Admiral Sir John Kelly, who restored discipline to the fleet, certainly provided a much needed and quite unofficial bridge between the c-in-c and the lower deck. Indeed Kelly's strictures on the Board of Admiralty's conduct, which caused them such pain, no doubt echoed many of Reggie's impressions of the sailor's views which he passed on to Kelly. The fact that in those days naval chaplains wore no uniform and had no rank was never more justified.

And so suddenly Reggie appeared in front of us, late, one morning to take prayers. To begin with we thought him a bit of a joke. He was apt to forget the time and, when he did turn up, the prayers he read were often new to us. He produced meditations which at first baffled us too. Deprecating compulsory sunday church (which meant removing and then replacing the mess tables before lunch), but conceding that king's regulations required that church should be held, he sought for variants to penetrate our hangovers. On a couple of sundays each month he would hold normal matins and preach a short but usually well worthwhile sermon. On other sundays he would lure one of his friends to talk to us. So we heard Dennis Wheatley on black magic, Ben Travers on farce, Ivor Brown, Gerald Heard and many others including a Benedictine monk. They contributed not at all to our knowledge of engineering or theology, but opened up new and hitherto unsuspected worlds. During our leaves Reggie took us to parts of England of unbelievable squalor and misery. He sat us at the feet of Dick Sheppard at St Martin-in-the-Fields, led us to help at the Heritage Craft Homes where Dame Agnes Kimmins supervised dozens of crippled children whose cheerfulness and courage were an inspiration. Over stupefying flagons of sherry, when we should have been studying mechanics, he would needle us on our beliefs and tell us of his.

Faith, he would say, *is reason standing on tiptoe. You must try and peer over the wall of disbelief which surrounds us all.* But his main message was always the same, *Develop a divine discontent with the* world as you find it. *Never be an iconoclast and pull down but build, build, build. Seek out how to be constructive: that is the message of the Gospels. Always be suspicious of tradition. Try to nurture and sustain and live up to it but never live only on it. The navy,* he rubbed into us, *is a living entity. At Invergordon it nearly died. You must help to revive it. Discipleship, discipline, is a matter of a man's spirit. Precision of drill and performance of evolutions is not the real way forward. Discipline demands pride of service. Officers have to show the way. The world is changing. The navy must change. Engineers must change. Society will change.*

Backed by Berthon and others, Reckless Reggie helped us in our search for wider understanding to prize open that door on the outside world Dartmouth had slammed shut. When, after world war two, ecclesiastical reactionaries infamously stopped his progress towards chaplain of the fleet, his beloved sovereign, King George VI with Queen Elizabeth, now the Queen Mother, took Reggie to Windsor as their chaplain.

After four years of hard play, work and (for me) even harder examinations I went back to sea. During that period Keyham had changed and we with it. Unknowingly there had been bred in most of us the stuff of technological revolution. But the world outside had altered. Indeed our very commissions were symptomatic of change. Our date for promotion to commissioned rank fell during the last days of the reign of King George V but our commissions were gazetted during the uncrowned reign of Edward VIII and eventually signed by King George VI.

Towards the end of my time at Keyham I had been asked whether I would join a New Zealand cruiser refitting at Devonport for service in the West Indies, which offer I naturally and enthusiastically accepted. Not for the last time the Almighty took a hand. The New Zealand government jibbed at paying for an officer under training. At that moment a sub-lieutenant (E) in *HMS Hood* who had developed conscientious objections to war resigned and I relieved him. As my very own old picket boat steamed past the Sally Port and Old Portsmouth the magnificent vista of the great fleets anchored at Spithead ready for the Coronation review was revealed. At the head of one line lay the *Hood*. It was like coming home.

CHAPTER 4

HMS *Hood* again, 1937-1939

A life on the ocean wave.   A home on the rolling deep.
Epes Sargent

THE JOURNEY FROM THE dockyard to the great assembly of ships for the Coronation review re-awakened something that had slept during my Keyham years.   Here, once more, was the navy and a ship I knew and loved.   Although I had only one stripe on my arm, this time I stumbled up the gangway far more confidently than when as a cadet I had first boarded her five years earlier.   As so often happens at moments of joy or excitement, there came a major put down.   The commander, chancing to be on the quarter-deck, welcomed me warmly but then asked, *Are you another of these pacifist subs from Keyham?*

I replied firmly in the negative, but it was an inauspicious start and it was clear I had something to live down.   Nevertheless to rejoin a ship and work below decks, after 15 months in the same ship as a very small cog in the world of executive command, was a major turning point in my naval life.

With some trepidation I entered the gunroom door at the ˙armchair end reserved for sub-lieutenants.   The brass stove, which I had so assiduously polished, was still there and to my delight I was welcomed by a near contemporary as the co-ruler of his little kingdom.   I soon discovered that the gunroom was still a place where laughter mostly prevailed and the food as bad as ever with the same grinning, but now even more pear-shaped, messman peering through the serving hatch;   where the same tin lockers in which I had kept my journal and sight book were still used by the midshipmen; where the only daylight came from the skylight. The same leather-coated cushions on the benches at the ship's side were even more worn as were the two leather armchairs of which I could now claim one.

My cabin, a small hutch below the armoured belt and therefore devoid of daylight, opened onto the flat where once I had slung my hammock. The gunroom bathroom still contained the large tank into which I had been taught to admit steam to provide hot water for the sub-lieutenants' baths, practically the only engineering I had absorbed before Keyham. On my first morning the bathwater was cold. Observing that the apologetic midshipman responsible had already suffered the statutory punishment from the other sub-lieutenant, I let him into the secret of how to heat the water quickly in an emergency. This established my apparent engineering omniscience and personal sympathy. Thereafter my bathwater was always hot.

Besides me, the newly joined trainee, there were 10 qualified engineers. The Commander (E) (the Chief) was a cherubic little man with a stutter which grew worse when he was angry. His number two (the senior engineer or more commonly, the Senior) had been the chief of *HMS Forres* the coal-fired sloop in which we had sicked our way for a week around the south coast during our last terms at Dartmouth. There were eight watchkeepers, four of them lieutenants (E) plus three warrant engineers (ex artificers) and one warrant mechanician. The mechanician scheme was another Fisher legacy for stokers with above average brains. Rather looked down upon by the artificers who entered the navy after quite a difficult written examination the mechanician certainly made up in experience and maturity for what he may have lacked in craft skills. Both types were indispensable. On my first morning the senior took me into all the machinery spaces including numerous glory holes known as cabooses, mostly housing ventilation machinery. But throwing open one caboose door he let me take a glance at five whey-faced elderly men in blue overalls, each holding a glass.

Those five chief engine room artificers (Ch ERAs), Maycock, Bradfield, Edmiston, Snell and Hemmings, he said *are among the most senior skilled men we have. I know, and they know, they have no right to be drinking prairie oysters of rum and raw eggs in the forenoon but they would give their lives for this ship. If we had to go to sea in an* emergency it would be their skills on which we would depend. Listen to them, learn from them and never mind asking them anything. If, after six months, when you come to get your watchkeeping ticket, you know a quarter of what they do about this ship,you will have·done well. If, when we get to Malta,they ask you to the ERA's club you must leave on your feet although overflowing with beer, and you will have won your spurs.

There were others of equal calibre: Mechanician Chilvers of the evaporators, Ridgeon of the steam picket boats, ERA Brading (later a commander (E)) and Chief ERA Edwards of the motor boats. Chief Stoker Biggenden slaved away with two registers in the stuffy engineer's office, one recording, inter alia, the actual oil fuel consumption and the other permitted consumption.   The latter, kept uniquely for the inspection of the fleet engineer officer showed, mysteriously, that we abided strictly by the rules, whatever the true facts.   How the books were reconciled was neither sought nor divulged.   Then there was Chief Stoker Watson who had started as a stoker when *Hood* first commissioned and was the only man to have visited each of her 1000 watertight compartments.   And Chief Stoker Abbott who, from an office the size of a British Rail gents, watched paternally over 300 stokers.

The royal review subordinated us all to smartening the ship and entertaining guests. Before the royal yacht *Victoria and Albert* progressed round the fleet, cheered by each ship in turn, we donned our cocked hats, frock coats, epaulettes, white gloves and swords and assembled on the lower signal bridge in strict Navy List order. This placed me at the end of the line of engineers, just ahead of the paymaster-commander.   Both he and the commander (E), a few paces to my right, were finding their cocked hats tight.   Neither's temper was improved during the long wait by the sound of popping corks as the admiral and his staff on the admiral's bridge above celebrated, with champagne, his new knighthood.

It had been intimated that I should take responsibility for *Hood's* 11 steam and power boats normally stowed on the boat deck.   I was sad to find that the magnificent steam barge I had known as a midshipman was soon to be replaced by a three-engined speedboat designed by Vospers. The story was that the soon-to-be Vice Admiral Sir Geoffrey Blake had insisted that after the review the new barge should take him to the royal yacht to receive his accolade.   This left no time for Peter Du Cane, once a commander (E), now a famous boatbuilder and director of Vospers, to carry out trials. From the boat deck I watched the new barge come alongside and heard the awful mechanical crunch when the coxswain went astern. With two engines only now serviceable the odds favoured the admiral getting to the royal yacht on time but alas it was not to be. The coxswain, anxious to show off the boat's speed, opened up both throttles to the maximum whereupon the engines died. Happily for the admiral, if not for Vospers, a yellow speed boat belonging to a rival firm spotted the disaster and delivered him to the royal yacht with only minutes to spare. Poor Peter Du Cane and his splendid firm were damned forever in the admiral's eyes but the beautiful old steam barge returned to the ship!

Thanks to good teachers I was awarded my engine room watchkeeping certificate in four, rather than the normal six, months. My responsibility for boats ended as dramatically as it had begun. Sir Geoffrey Blake suffered a mild heart attack and was relieved by Rear Admiral Andrew Cunningham who lost no time in coming out to Malta. Early one morning Sir Geoffrey's flag lieutenant took the barge to meet Cunningham's liner and ascertain the time of his formal arrival on board his new flagship. For some reason I was on the quarterdeck about 0820 when the barge rounded our stern and came alongside the starboard ladder, up which ran a somewhat rotund figure followed by a clearly hysterical flag lieutenant and a sailor laden with several suitcases. My comment to the officer of the watch, who was writing up the deck log in the lobby, *that in my day as a seaman it was usual for the officer of the watch, at least, to meet an admiral,* was treated as a poor joke. But when I suggested that the small man in mufti must surely be Admiral Cunningham, a scene ensued to which only H M Bateman could have done justice. The captain was in his bath, the commander breakfasting in the wardroom, the admiral's secretary in his bunk with his morning cup of tea, while the admiral, delighted at outwitting his flagship, was changing into uniform and admiring his magnificent quarters.

With everybody's nerves taut as bowstrings, it was not long before the beautiful steam barge was called away to take Cunningham to pay his respects to the Commander-in-Chief, Admiral Sir Dudley Pound. What possessed the admiral's coxswain, a rather grand chief petty officer who conversed normally only with the admiral's staff, I shall never know but just as he was about to leave the starboard quarterboom he saw the admiral descending to the quarterdeck. Quickly he rang down for Full Ahead and, turning hard a-starboard in full view of the quarterdeck élite, placed the barge fair and square in the path of a picket boat. The barge was stove in just for'd of her boiler room and at first it seemed both boats might sink. It took 80 men on four guy ropes to work the *Hood's* main derrick and never before had they been assembled with such speed. The admiral, by now also steaming slightly, was dispatched in the captain's small motor boat to keep his appointment with the commander-in-chief.

It was during the trip from *Hood* to Custom House Jetty that Admiral Cunningham asked Lieutenant James Munn (later Rear-Admiral W J Munn CB, DSO, OBE), who had been Sir Geoffrey Blake's flag lieutenant, if he wished to remain as his 'Flags' and gave him 24 hours to decide. Inside that time Munn accepted adding, 'after all, sir, there must be many worse jobs than being your flag-lieutenant'. A comment ABC never let him forget.

When things had quietened down and the disgraced admiral's coxswain dispatched to the UK, the problem of his replacement arose. There were two options: the commander could second one of his best chief petty officers to the post or the second coxswain, a young leading seaman whom I unreservedly recommended, be given the job. Leading seaman Watts understood machinery, was on the best of terms with the engine and boiler room crew and, I had found, was always smart, keen and enthusiastic. As acting Chief and then Chief Petty Officer Watts he remained with the future Admiral of the Fleet, Viscount Cunningham of Hyndhope, throughout the war in which ABC was to make his name as our greatest fighting admiral since Nelson.

The four months' training time had made me realise that although *Hood* was a reasonably happy ship Captain A F Pridham and Commander David Orr-Ewing had had considerable difficulties to overcome. In the previous commission *Hood* had spent too long in Gibraltar with little for the sailors to do. Discipline had slipped and the wardroom felt that Commander O'Conor, Orr-Ewing's predecessor, had over-trimmed his scale of punishments. He was inclined, it was said, to treat sailors who were part of the ship's sports teams more leniently if they offended than the rest of the ship's company. Furthermore, early in the commission, there had been an extraordinary collision between *Hood* and *Renown* seriously damaging both ships and resulting in courts-martial, including that of the admiral. Unfortunately O'Conor took the fact that *Renown* hit *Hood* (it might well have been the other way round) as a personal insult; never again would he board *Renown*. So the happy battle cruiser spirit that Admiral James had built up during my midshipman's time was wholly dissipated.

Captain Pridham had relieved Captain Tower who, with Commander O'Conor, had originally recommissioned *Hood* in 1933 whilst I was still in her as a midshipman. For some time Pridham had to live with the O'Conor commission and a ship in a state of discipline he found unsatisfactory. After a few months *Hood* partially recommissioned and many of the O'Conor veterans left while Commander Orr-Ewing relieved O'Conor. Pridham and Orr-Ewing, outwardly austere men, held strong views on discipline and soon a better atmosphere began to prevail. As I came to realise after a few months, both, under a rather grim carapace, had warmth and professional expertise. To this, in Pridham's case, was added an unequalled ability to handle a great ship. Unfortunately Pridham had also to cope with the intense dislike of the Commander-in-Chief, Admiral Sir Dudley Pound. For many years I carried around Pridham's *Captain's memorandum on discipline* which was a far more down-to-earth document than the Admiralty memorandum on *Disaffection* issued by Dudley Pound when he was Second Sea Lord and Chief of Naval Personnel. Sadly this clash of views as to how discipline should be maintained was the main *casus belli* between these two great men. Their mutual distrust was not improved when, on a foggy day in full view of the commander-in-chief, *Hood* straddled *HMS Protector* with a 15-in salvo instead of a target she was towing. Happily for the navy the gunnery officer's promotion was signalled that evening and he went on to become a famous admiral, as indeed did his deputy who rather unjustly received Their Lordship's displeasure for a mistake which was not his direct responsibility.

The arrival of Commander (E) C P Berthon as our new chief brought to the engineering department a man whose views on discipline were similar to those of Pridham and Orr-Ewing. Like them he was not pleased with what he found when he joined, but he was quick to realise that the vast old ship for whose 144,000 shaft horsepower and much other machinery he was responsible, was a different cup of tea from the cruiser in which he had served before his recent appointment to Keyham. As the senior engineer soon concluded a new, dynamic mind was a great help to us all.

In those days *HMS Ganges*, the boys training establishment, was perhaps the most effective machine ever invented for turning often scruffy adolescents into fine young seamen, to strengthen both the navy and later the state when their engagement ended. That this superlative training was never extended to stokers recruited straight from the coal mines was a naval aberration.

Traditionally in *Hood* a newly qualified (E) officer was given an engineering department to supervise where he could do least harm. As it seemed likely that I would be the only commissioned officer whose relief was not planned for the months ahead, Berthon put me in charge of *Hood's* 24 boilers and the associated machinery with a newly promoted warrant engineer as assistant. He also made me responsible for the training of the younger stokers and artificers whose first duty was always in the boiler rooms. He acknowledged 10 years later when I became his son-in-law, that he saw this as a case of 'the blind leading the blind'. Nevertheless he judged, perhaps correctly, that a young commissioned officer might communicate more effectively than an old hard-bitten warrant engineer with the willing, but mainly untrained and rather undisciplined, ex-miners who staffed the boiler rooms.

Half a century ago, particularly in world war one-designed ships, boiler feed water was rarely pure. To prevent corrosion of boiler drums and tubes it was frequently necessary, depending on sea time , to remove all heat-insulating lagging, open up each boiler, clean and blacklead the internal fittings and then, through a small manhole, perform the same rites inside each of the three boiler drums, brushing through every tube. By dropping carefully counted balls down each of several thousand individual tubes we ensured that there was no blockage which, when steaming, could inhibit the water's circulation and cause the tube to melt and explode into the furnace with probable casualties. Leading stoker bricklayers with their unskilled mates would be breaking up damaged fire brick walls in the furnace and removing the rubble before building and cementing new ones. Yet another gang would be inserting 10ft saws between the tubes to remove soot and clinker and sweeping down and oiling the inside of *Hood's* huge funnels. Meantime artificers and mechanicians would be refitting steam, water and oil valves, repairing steam leaks, resetting safety valves and refitting associated auxiliary machinery. Finally each boiler would be pumped up to its working pressure and tested for leaks. With 24 boilers in four boiler rooms this job was never ending. Asbestosis had not been heard of and we all lived for long hours in a fog of brick dust, asbestos fibre and soot. Work went on round the clock in six- or eight-hour spells, depending on the heat and urgency, until completed.

Captain Pridham's turnover notes for his successor included, *Like many good looking ladies* Hood *is inclined to be wilful and likes surprising you. If she gets up to mischief give her a good hard thump with the engines and helm and she will immediately behave like a perfect lady - she responds to a heavy hand when she knows she has deserved it.* This meant constant alertness, considerable dexterity and unremitting attention to detail by the young stokers.

The chief stoker was 'orchestral' conductor in a boiler room usually at a temperature of 90°F-100°F, dimly lit by shockproof lamps and the flickering of furnace flames. Fans supplying air for combustion made normal conversation impossible and ears popped badly with 10 inches or more of varying air pressure. While controlling the steam to the fans, the chief stoker would keep his eye both on a periscope to watch for funnel smoke, and the steam to the oil fuel pumps whose speed was related to the number, up to eight, of sprayers on each boiler. This he would orchestrate by hitting a shell case with a spanner to attract each boiler operator's attention and manually indicate whether to open up and flash further sprayers or shut them and close the air flaps. Incorrect operation by a single stoker (and when the Malta gregale wind was blowing *Hood* sometimes needed all 24 boilers) could cause smoke to billow from the funnels; or if sprayers were shut slowly as the turbine throttles were closed, the safety valves would lift with a roar heard all over Malta. If however the throttles on the turbines were opened fast to give her a good hard thump, and the sprayers were not opened fast enough, steam could be lost, leaving the main engines and dynamos powerless, the ship motionless and in darkness.

Those who have boiled over milk in a saucepan are only too aware of the froth that spills onto the stove. Similarly, automatic valves regulate the water level when more sprayers are opened and heat is applied(as water level rises so supply cuts off) or sprayers are shut and heat reduced (water level falls so supply opens up). There was one watchkeeper to every three boilers by the water gauge glasses, as any failure of the automatic water regulators required an instantaneous changeover to hand operation or a major disaster, with casualties, would ensue.

Berthon's answer to Pridham's dissatisfaction with our smoke was to give me the task of raising stoker morale and perfecting our sprayer drill to bring *Hood* to her buoys without enveloping Valetta in smog. I was fortunate that the boys' divisional officer was a friend and willing adviser. First we removed all the younger stokers from those messes where they were apt to be influenced by a few bad hats, and gave them their own mess with a good leading stoker in charge. Next we started evening classes for stokers and young artificers to relate their work to the running of the ship. We secured Pridham's permission to station a few on the bridge structure when he took *Hood* in and out of harbour. Here they could see (and sometimes experience) the inadvertent smoke screen and begin to understand ship handling. Best of all the boy's divisional officer agreed that for banyan (picnic) parties, the young stokers could join his boys. The money allowed for coach tours at the ports we visited he kindly shared between the two groups. Obvious enough now perhaps, but 50 years ago in big ships there was an even greater gap between stokers and seamen than between (E) and executive officers. Productivity and efficiency in boiler operation and cleaning increased dramatically. There were even requests, some granted, from boy seamen and young Royal Marines to change over to stoker!

No musician myself I was fortunate that Chief Stoker Cathmoir was an expert mouth organ player. He gathered around him 20 stoker harmonica players, as well as several, including a shipwright (now Commander C T Haynes OBE), who were talented accordeon players. Canteen committee funds fitted them out with natty uniforms in *Hood* colours. My task was that of fixtures secretary, shepherd and general peacemaker, but it was Cathmoir who kept *Hood's Harmony Boys* on the road for increasingly sophisticated performances. Unfortunately their success landed me with another chore, that of ship's dance officer, but of that more later.

While in Malta junior members of the fleet wardrooms divided into two groups. There were those who sought the fishing fleet, charming girls brought to Malta by their mothers in the hope of ensnaring some up-and-coming young naval or army officer: and there were those who preferred, or were financially constrained to, bachelordom. The former required smart civilian

• *Hood's Harmony Boys. Shipwright Haynes (back row, far right). Author, next row, fifth, Lt Cdr (E) L Fogg-Elliott, seventh and Chief Stoker Cathmoir sixth from right*

clothes, engraved calling cards and the wherewithal to entertain these delicious creatures. Happily for me my boilers, my involvement in *Hood's Harmony Boys*, the ship's dance committee and hockey side together with a half share in a polo pony indicated which path perforce I must follow.

For a few pounds one could play some rather amateur polo early of a summer's morning, and on some saturday afternoons. The admiral, no opera lover, occasionally bequeathed his opera house box to the wardroom. Usually the senior engineer, Lancelot Fogg-Elliott, too busy on board to be anything but a bachelor, would dine with us weekly at Valletta's Union Club. This had a men-only entrance, but through a peep-hole one could jealously watch the poodle-fakers as they disported themselves with their damsels in the presence of some rather forbidding looking mothers. From frustrated voyeurism it was but a step to the long bar and a gimlet (still the in-drink) and so to the magnificent room, where the knights of Malta had once dined, and an excellent but economic meal.

Sunday divisions and church were obligatory but, unless there was a sailor's picnic, the bachelor's routine was invariable: change into old clothes, pack bathing gear and take a dghaisa to the Sliema Club, (equally sex divided). There on Monkey Island we could laze, sustained by cheap gin, a blistering curry, followed by blessed sleep on the warm rocks, a bathe and lustful discussions on the poodle-fakers and their companions' physical attributes

30 yards across the channel of water. Then iced almond cake for tea and a slow dghaisa back to the wardroom cinema.

Visits to the Western Mediterranean and the war zone were more serious periods broken by glorious days at Golfe Juan and Tangier. Anxious to show how well (E) officers could sail, the gunroom bet the wardroom they could take a cutter from Tangier to Gibraltar between dawn and dusk. Impossible, said the navigator, because of the strong westerly current on the Tangier side. Current was indeed the main problem and required that the cutter should not be driven by it too far towards America before catching the east-setting flow along the Spanish coast. As dawn broke we set off and were greatly heartened by a vast Italian liner which dipped her ensign to the white ensign I had illegally hoisted at the gaff. Fortunately an afternoon breeze sprang up and we passed Gibraltar breakwater just as *Hood's* bugler was inflating his lungs for sunset. Six of us from the gunroom had a splendid blow out at the Rock Hotel; and the wardroom paid.

Italy still occupied Abyssinia and Palestine was simmering, while the dreadful cruelties of the Spanish Civil War were being enacted at the other end of the Mediterranean. Admiral Cunningham had been relieved by Admiral Layton and Captain Pridham by Captain 'Hooky' Walker who, as a result of the storming of Zeebrugge in world war one, had a brass gaff instead of his left forearm which struck terror into defaulters as he banged it on the table. But he and his wife quickly found their way to our hearts, as did the Laytons and their glamorous daughters.

Before Chamberlain returned from Munich to proclaim peace in our time *Hood* had sailed into the Atlantic to do battle with our friends in the *Deutchland*, whose wounded we had tended when she was bombed and hit at Palma. She was said to be lying in wait to destroy the *Aquitania* bringing troops and reinforcements to the Mediterranean. I had a viciously high temperature from an infected graze on the Gibraltar hockey pitch and remember tossing and turning through a disturbed night as the warheads were brought up from the magazines below the sickbay and attached to the torpedoes. To the surgeon commander's surprise, for antibiotics were then unknown, the excitement brought my temperature back to normal and I was able to resume my place on the watchbill.

After Munich we returned to Gibraltar as did the *Deutchland* and with the exception of the admiral who had suffered from the

• *En route by cutter to Gibraltar from Tangier. Hood was always a wet ship as bottles under the Author's arms confirm*

Germans in world war one, resumed our friendships. The beer, which the German ship carried in such quantities, we particularly appreciated.

In Malta a few days before Christmas 1938, we heard the ship would return home early in the new year for a major refit. The canteen committee promptly demanded a great paying-off dance in Portsmouth, to which the captain and commander acceded depositing its arrangement in my lap. An officer in his department had been given a responsibility affecting the ship's company and reputation so my chief relieved me of all engineering duties and bade me get on with it.

From then until we left Malta I spent my time in continuous session with the ship's dance committee or ashore in the Cable and Wireless office. The lord mayor of Portsmouth was massively helpful and the lovely old Guildhall was booked for what was one of its last great functions before Hitler destroyed it. The equation between what number of tickets would be sold at what cost, how much we could afford to pay the band and the scale of eating and drinking, an integral part of any ship's dance, was not easy to solve. There was an increasingly hysterical series of telegrams to Brickwoods the famous Portsmouth brewery who were to do the catering. The last one before we sailed for England summed it all up; *Cancel savoury brioche, substitute strawberry ice cream. Cannot exceed two shillings and sixpence per head for guaranteed 2000.*

After a last farewell to my little polo pony and the small dinghy I had somehow acquired, we sailed home, our long paying off pennant flying from the masthead and the bladder on its end dancing in our wake.

CHAPTER 5

To war

The dark bitter waters are rising fast on either side.
Winston Churchill, House of Commons, April 13 1939

WITH THE SHIP'S COMPANY DANCE behind me I was allocated to the hackwork of refit and came to realise *Hood's* unfitness for war. There were many major defects besides her thin deck armour. Due to extra anti-aircraft armament, ammunition and crew to man it plus the tons of paint applied during *Hood's* 20 years showing the flag, the ship was a foot further down in the water than her designed draught. In anything but a flat calm, waves now broke over the quarterdeck and salt water penetrated, corroded and immobilised the roller path of 'Y' 15in turret thus reducing main firepower by 25%. The thickness of the paint between decks also constituted a major fire hazard.

To reduce weight and bring the ship up to her designed draught it had been intended to remove all 10 of *Hood's* 5.5in guns secondary armament and associated ammunition. This would enable the installation of thicker deck armour and a more sophisticated anti-aircraft outfit. But with war in the air such major work would have prevented the ship rejoining the fleet quickly; so only a major paint removal drive was judged feasible.

The other nightmare affecting the ship's mobility was the feed water's worsening impurity which corroded our boilers. The tubes in the ship's main condensers under the great turbines were aged and rotting. Salt sea water drawn by vacuum into the condensing steam contaminated the water on its way back to the boiler, a constant problem in ships during world war one known as 'condenseritis'. In addition the reserve boiler feed water tanks in the double bottoms were leaking at their seams, causing more contamination. And these two problems fed on each other. When the boiler water became contaminated it was necessary to ditch it and replenish supplies from the evaporators which were sometimes of insufficient capacity to cope with the amount needing replacement. Then water, probably contaminated, had to be pumped from the reserve tanks. To the engineer-in-chief's department the *Engineering Manual* was sacred. Routine inspections but no work outside the scope of our attenuated ship's staff was to be undertaken. Commander (E) Berthon, prone on occasion to white-hot shaking rages, returned from one meeting in London incandescent.

Two events confirmed the immediacy of war. In March 1939 Professor Lewis Namier told an audience of sceptical senior officers (to which I had been sent to make up numbers), *Hitler is now ready to march against Poland but he will not do so until the harvest is in. I predict that you will be at war with Germany by the beginning of September.*

Then, just as *Hood* was being towed from dock to jetty, an Admiralty signal warned us to expect air raids. With only stokers on board we quickly procured some ammunition and, with the help of a gunner's mate from *HMS Excellent*, tried to show our unskilled but martial band which end of the AA guns the shells went in.

Our senior left to become chief of *HMS Galatea* and was relieved by Lieutenant-Commander (E) John Erskine. Eventually Berthon, steadfastly refusing to sign a certificate that *Hood* was in a seaworthy let alone a battleworthy state, was relieved by Commander (E) Terence Grogan, famed for racing his Bentley at Brooklands .

Machinery spares, boiler bricks, oaken shores, jointing by the mile, extra hoses . . . day and night merged as we strove to make up for a decade's neglect. Disparity widened between what had to be done and the blazing irrelevancies Admiralty poured on us. Endless hours were spent cajoling officials torn between instincts and orders. When finally we sailed to war all Portsmouth and Southsea turned out to cheer farewell to a great ship, one they would never see again.

We had often practised darkening ship but it had always ended before midnight so that scuttles and hatches could be reopened to admit fresh air. This humid August evening permitted no such relaxation. German submarines were at sea and our departure surely known; a torpedo might strike at any time. Tension and, perhaps, fear added to the stinking heat permeating the ill-ventilated messdecks. We tried to alleviate the fug by drawing air through the ship to the boiler rooms but this involved opening too many watertight doors. For officers the situation was equally unpleasant: what had been the best cabins under the quarterdeck were abandoned and shut off. Those of us with previously less desirable residences behind the armoured belt now had to yield them to our seniors and take to camp beds in passages.

Early one morning, still sleepy and unused to the discomfort that was to become routine, we passed the boom defence vessel into the safety of Scapa Flow as we innocently assumed, just six years after my little *Horizon* had bucketed her way into the Pentland Firth. Within days we were off into the Atlantic with the Home Fleet and destroyer escort. I was on watch in the great cathedral of *Hood's* forward controlling engine room when a messenger brought me the signal, *Total Germany,* which meant 'Commence hostilities' against Germany. A few hours later the *Athenia,* with many children among her passengers, was sunk by U-boat: unrestricted submarine warfare had started. Then came the signal, *Winston is back* to encourage us all.

Damage control, a new phrase to us, spawned a more comprehensive organisation than the old 'Fire and repair parties' ever did. Essentially technical, it should have been under the direction of an engineer or shipwright officer, but in those days no (E) officer could give orders to shipwrights or sailors and no artificer, mechanician or stoker would take them from a chippie. So the first lieutenant whose knowledge of pumping, flooding, shoring, the cross connecting of damaged fire or hydraulic mains and the running of emergency electrical leads could have been written on a postage stamp, had perforce to become the damage control supremo, all orders being issued over his name.

Strict discipline had to be exercised in the closing of watertight doors and hatches. Just how essential this was came home to us a few days later when *HMS Courageous* was torpedoed with considerable loss of life. All watertight doors were shut below

Hood's main deck so restricting movement that a trip to the heads in the bows became virtually impossible. Makeshift sanitary arrangements of doubtful efficacy had to be employed.

For engineer officers wartime watchkeeping routine was much as in peacetime, one watch in three. But for our executive messmates who in peacetime had kept a bridge watch of about one in 16 the shock was immense. Much of the main, secondary and anti-aircraft armament had now to be kept ready for action which reduced the executive branch to our sort of watch routine. When we were not carrying out the disagreeable chore of censoring letters, and with only a few cabins available at sea the wardroom quickly became full of sleepy and often crotchety recumbent figures.

By now I had been offered an appointment to the battleship *King George V*, then building on the Tyne, or a small *Dido* class cruiser *Naiad* (which I preferred) shortly to complete at Hawthorn Leslie's Yard on the same river. Awaiting my translation with a roving commission to help the newly joined first lieutenant, I temporarily became *Hood's* upper deck damage control officer and I saw action for the first time. Late in September 1939 a damaged British submarine, *HMS Spearfish,* was crawling back home across the North Sea. Cruisers and destroyers were dispatched to escort her with a covering force consisting of *Nelson, Rodney* and *Ark Royal* to the north, and *Hood* and *Royal Oak* to the south, both groups in sight of each other. As the *Ark Royal* had recently been near-missed by a torpedo there was considerable tension. Having met *Spearfish* we turned for home whereupon two shadowing aircraft appeared well out of gun range. *Ark Royal* kept her fighters on deck anticipating the arrival of German bombers.

Lieutenant-Commander 'Tiny' Gregson, the *Hood's* gunnery officer, conceived a magisterial rebuke to the shadowers. One of *Hood's* after turrets was told to load both 15in guns with shrapnel shells, a few of which *Hood* carried for shore bombardment. No hits were obtained, but there was a spectacular explosion on the horizon and thereafter the shadowers kept their distance. In due course the bombers came in from the north and *Ark Royal's* fighters were scrambled. For some reason, probably sheer panic and confusion, *Nelson's* port battery opened fire on the wrong side (southwards) towards *Hood*, happily without damaging us. The bombers struck at *Ark Royal* and, although they scored no hits, vast waterspouts hid her from our sight.

The gun's crews on *Hood's* boatdeck, as well as my damage control party, were watching the attack on *Ark Royal* when a bomb, seemingly the size of a grand piano, fell out of the sun to the south of us towards the boatdeck, a few feet short. A frightening explosion alongside opened up the top of the anti-torpedo bulge and the port lower boom was shredded with splinters. All the hot and cold water pipes in the stoker's bathroom, abreast the explosion, fractured. But more serious was the loss of electrical power to the port eight-barrelled pom-pom. A circuit breaker had been knocked off by the shock. The electrical repair parties were defeated by *Hood's* past: brass information plates on the junction boxes detached for polishing had been muddled when replaced. Efforts to run emergency power leads to the pom-pom succeeded only in bringing some warmth to the petty officer's hot locker, not materially adding to our fighting potential. Lord Haw-Haw, as the traitorous voice of the Berlin propaganda broadcasts was now called, announced that both *Ark Royal* and *Hood* had been sunk. That they were not was due more to an inscrutable providence than to our gunnery or fighters. On this the fleet's first encounter with air power no bombers were shot down.

Routine tests then revealed a near-critical contamination of the boiler feed water. Some tubes and tube joints had failed: we were in for a severe dose of condenseritis. Happily our predecessors had discovered a bizarre method of rendering first aid. Valves on the seawater side of the condenser permitted the injection of sawdust from hoppers. The condenser vacuum, which had been drawing in seawater through leaky joints or pinholes in the corroded tubes, also drew in grains of sawdust which temporarily plugged the leaks. None of us had seen this used, but if we were to reach Scapa without irreparable boiler damage we had to try it out speedily. Our shipwrights, luckily, already had some bags of sawdust and soon their bandsaws started producing more. To our surprise the medicine worked and *Hood* reached Scapa safely.

Once at anchor the complex testing of condensers began: although the portside condensers were worst effected, there was trouble in all four. Then we met another snag. The condenser designers had had the prescience to fit sawdust hoppers, but had underestimated the space between condenser tube plates and the outer casing. Sadly the navy does not recruit midgets, so we turned instead to ERA Wigfall our smallest artificer. Clad in a bathing slip Wigfall crept into the worst condenser to tighten the joints and plug the leaking tubes. We kept him going with draughts of hot Shovril, increasing the proportion of sherry to hot Bovril as his weariness increased. Thanks to his 24-hour slog we were able to report readiness for sea but with restrictions on speed which galled our chief, Terence Grogan. Thenceforward Wigfall was given a high protein diet so that his dimensions would not increase coupled with light duties when we were not in harbour. I can see him now as we lifted him out of the small manhole, his lips blue, his teeth chattering. For some weeks *Hood's* warfighting and operational capability rested on Wigfall's thin shoulders. Somehow we kept her at sea, but after six weeks *Hood's* maximum speed was down to 27 knots and we knew that if that speed was prolonged, condenseritis would recur.

In October, in the worst weather yet, we were off the Lofoten Islands escorting a precious convoy of iron ore from Narvik. The messdecks grew colder, and the ship's steam heating (never before used) leaked so badly that it had to be shut off as the evaporators could not make up the water lost. Continuous rolling and pitching caused the deck joints between the great armoured conning tower and the upper deck to leak so badly that running water on the messdecks added to the miseries of overcrowding and cold. Respite came with occasional visits to Loch Ewe, on the west coast of Scotland, where air raid alarms were less frequent than in Scapa. We also felt safer from submarine attack, such as had just sunk *Royal Oak* in the Flow. Constant pounding was tiring the old hull even more than the ship's company. Condenser leaks were now a fact of life; the working of the ship's bottom plates worsened the leaks into the reserve feed tanks, as predicted. Boiler cleaning, due to excessive seatime and contaminated water, became never-ending. Machinery maintenance increased daily as Berthon's prophecies came home to roost at the Admiralty.

In Grogan, the chief, and Erskine, the senior, we had superlative leaders who for another four months kept the ship at sea until the work that should have been undertaken in 1939 could be put in hand. Dartmouth had drummed into me that what the Admiralty said or did was always right, now I came to realise that often they were entirely wrong. It was the start of a lengthy awakening. Churchill came on board while I was still in *Hood* and Grogan told him of the sawdust answer to our problem. Grogan's view then was that we could keep going for another six months. At that time we were all optimists and expected the war to fizzle out once Hitler realised that his blockade was not paying off.

After sorties in October and early November *Hood* was sent to Devonport, to give the first real shore leave since quitting Portsmouth three months earlier. As we rounded Land's End a signal ordered me to report forthwith to the Admiral Superintendent, Contract Built Ships in Newcastle. Although both wardroom and gunroom contained many delightful people with whom I had become fast friends, I was conscious that I had been in *Hood* overlong too apt, now, to look back to earlier and easier days. I spent some of my remaining hours touring the ship. It was a sad if, in the chief stoker's, artificer's and chief petty officer's messes, a singularly alcoholic parting which the wardroom completed: I was thankful for the taxi that bore me to North Road Station.

* * * * *

Seventeen months later, in April 1941, *HMS Naiad* anchored close to *Hood* in Scapa Flow. The midshipmen for whose engineering instruction I had been responsible, had just passed for sub-lieutenant and were celebrating their success and departure for courses and requested my assistance. Hearing that I had accepted, Erskine invited me to supper after the gunroom had finished with me. When leaving I found a couple of dozen or so of the ship's company, not all from the engine department, waiting to say goodbye and to wish me luck. Who arranged this, I shall never know. In less than six weeks they all were dead.

CHAPTER 6

The building of *HMS Naiad*

Stand by. The lull 'twixt blast and blast
Signals the storm is near, not past.
And worse than present jeopardy
May our forlorn tomorrow be.
The Storm Cone Rudyard Kipling

THE TRANSITION FROM life at sea with its constant alarms, the enervating engine room heat and the high-pitched scream of fans to the comfort of Newcastle digs was bliss. Though mine was but a small part of the load carried by Grogan and Erskine, the struggle to keep a worn-out ship operational had been wearing and wearying. Apart from the black-out in London, through which I passed on leave, it was hard to tell the country was at war. Of the real struggle at sea there was little understanding: the battle of the River Plate and the *Graf Spee*'s destruction, encouraged the feeling that the navy was now on top of the German threat.

Newcastle, on the other hand, had a sense of purpose engendered by a labour-force formerly condemned to unemployment and the soup kitchen. Work was now plentiful as ships with storm, and sometimes battle, damage arrived to reawaken Tyneside. *HMS Naiad*, recently launched from Hawthorn Leslie's Hebburn yard, was having her machinery installed built by the same firm further up river. The shipyard itself across the Tyne from Wallsend, the final bastion of Hadrian s Wall built against the Picts some 1500 years earlier, was where now we left our cars and caught the morning ferry.

What men those Geordies were and doubtless still are. From chairman Robin Rowell, Chris Stevenson shipyard manager, Douglas

Ogilvie engine manager, through bowler-hatted foremen to fitters and shipwrights, they spared no effort to meet our importunate demands. Official overseers, if determined to keep within Admiralty rules and regulations, appreciated that it was we, not they, who would be going to war in the cruiser we were building together. Work went on by day and night in that bitter 1939/40 winter. Unforeseen crises prevented our accepting the invitations with which the hospitable Newcastle folk flooded us. On saturdays, however, at noon there was a gathering at the Heaton Corner House of most of the (E) officers standing by the Tyne-building ships, where we swapped common problems and their possible solutions. It was the same when we met the managers and foremen in the Eldon's upper bar, or our chiefs and petty officers in the Turk's Head and the Pineapple. Newcastle Breweries, like *Naiad*, certainly profited from our various discussions.

Despite hiccoughs Hawthorn Leslie's conscientious workforce always seemed to be able to surmount the frequent design anomalies that arose. But it was the rivet boys who set the pace. Few will ever forget Winkle, probably the original Bisto Kid. A cap too large for his small head and a patched jacket covering his thin frame, he looked about eight but was in fact nearly 16. In rain or snow he was always by his brazier with an almost identical brother working the bellows and feeding rivets. When Winkle judged a rivet to be at the correct heat, he would pick it out with his tongs and toss it through the air to a third brother who, in turn, caught it in a tin can, seized it with his tongs and pushed it through the rivet hole on the other side of which stood Winkle senior and his pneumatic hammer. With an apparently inexhaustible supply of rivets and energy Winkle set the pace, remonstrating with an enviable string of oaths when a rivet fell or the supply faltered. Occasionally he would swop places with his 'catcher' brother, but Winkle's tongue was rarely stilled and would come echoing up from some deck seam deep within the hull. Why he was called Winkle we never discovered but one thing was certain, Winkle was at war.

HMS Kelly, another Hawthorn Leslie product, was alongside refitting when a new German minefield, off the mouth of the Tyne, claimed two tankers. *Kelly*, helping to rescue survivors, then ran into a mine which blew off her stern. Next day she was towed back about five per cent shorter. A combination of Mountbatten charm and the Admiralty's need for destroyers slowed progress on *Naiad* despite more night work and overtime.   Even Winkle seemed to work faster.

Many British warships, for a variety of reasons, were 'short legged'.   An inexperienced bridge officer , too far astern or too close to the next ahead, might order an over-abrupt change in propeller revolutions, or an artificer opening or closing a throttle too quickly might concertina a whole line of ships.   Such variation squandered precious fuel and thus reduced an already attenuated range.   Mountbatten had invented a technically brilliant device to overcome this problem and *Naiad* was the first cruiser fitted with it.   I dared to ask him to explain its inner workings to our artificers so that we might maintain it, reduce wear and tear on our machinery and, thus, save fuel.   Enthusiastically he complied but the sequel was less happy.   When our admiral joined and our captain proudly told him we were the first cruiser to have the Mountbatten Station Keeping Gear the former, not a Mountbatten fan, purpled, *As station keeping was not a requirement for cruisers in wartime,* he said, *dismantle it at once and put it ashore.*   Thereafter we did little else but keep station on convoys or battle groups.   With an increasing proportion of enthusiastic if inexperienced RNVR officers on the bridge and increasingly inexperienced artificers on the throttles, we cursed our admiral by day and night.   Twenty years later, at Lord Mountbatten's request, I was instrumental in unearthing this particular model which he presented to the National Maritime Museum.

When *Kelly's* stern had been rebuilt Mountbatten and his wife gave a farewell party on board for the ship's company.   Lady Mountbatten, it was said, paid for all the wives to come to Hebburn.   Some of us from *Naiad* were asked as well.   When Mountbatten stood on *Kelly's* gangway and introduced each sailor by name to his own wife, without prompting, he was no different from any other destroyer captain with the wherewithal to throw such a party.   I first heard of the destroyer flotilla's spirit at Keyham.   At the time of the Invergordon mutiny Commodore D'Oyly Lyon and his wife had bought a house near us in Gloucestershire and occasionally I made up a foursome with him and his two sons.   One day the conversation turned to Invergordon and the reasons why there had been no hint of similar troubles in the Atlantic fleet flotillas then at Rosyth.   It came out that when the commodore was told of the lower pay scales he summoned all his commanding officers to the flagship, *Cairo,* and stopped leave until every man who wished to do so had written down precisely what the proposed pay cuts meant to him and his family. That night D'Oyly Lyon took the sleeper from Edinburgh and dumped the sack of letters in the office of the second sea lord (personnel) with the intimation that if the injustices were not remedied he would haul down his commodore's broad pennant. D'Oyly Lyon believed that the navy could never operate to its potential with a Board of Admiralty so manifestly out of touch with the lower deck. The type of personal leadership we saw in *Kelly* was general in the destroyer flotillas and was largely responsible for making them so formidable throughout six years of war.

Sadly for *Naiad's* completion date we had not seen the last of *Kelly*. In action with E-boats in the North Sea, she received a torpedo amidships when doing 29 knots and by all the rules should have sunk. Thanks largely to *HMS Bulldog* coupled with Mountbatten's ruthless disposal of topweight and Hawthorn Leslie's building skills *Kelly* was towed back up river and berthed alongside *Naiad* till she could be docked. As the water drained away we helped remove what little was left of *Kelly's* boiler room crew, soon to lie where they are today in Hebburn's quiet cemetery,

• *Kelly back at Newcastle after her engagement with E-boats*

• *The launch of Naiad*

and could see how well she had been built. From upper deck to keel plate there was a void with just two rivets holding together the two halves of the ship . We could only hope that Winkle had done as well with *Naiad*.

As details about the disastrous Norwegian campaign filtered through the battle for France reached its tragic climax, so graphically portrayed in the *New York Times'* issue of June 1,1940.

So long as the English tongue survives,the word Dunkirk will be spoken with reverence.For in that harbour, in such a hell as never blazed on earth before,at the end of a lost battle, the rags and blemishes that have hidden the soul of democracy fell away. There beaten but unconquered, in shining splendour she faced the enemy.

They sent away the wounded first. Men died so that others could escape. It was not so simple a thing as courage, which the Nazis had in plenty. It was not so simple a thing as discipline which can be hammered into men by a drill sergeant. It was not the result of careful planning, for there could have been little. It was the common man of the free countries, rising in all his glory out of mill, office, factory, mine, farm and ship, applying to war the lessons learned when he went down the shaft to bring out trapped comrades, when he hurled the lifeboat through the surf, when he endured poverty and hardwork for his children's sake.

This shining thing in the souls of free men Hitler cannot command, or attain or conquer. He has crushed it where he could in German hearts.

It is the great tradition of democracy. It is the future. It is victory.

Gradually, as some of the battered ships came to the Tyne, we began to hear the Dunkirk saga: six destroyers sunk, another 20 so damaged that they would be unserviceable for months whatever miracles the Winkles could perform.

Finally our commissioning day arrived and, with it, the balance of the ship's company together with our ammunition in barges. After stand-easy the captain decided to address the ship's company. As we gathered aft there was an air raid warning.

Let's get this stuff below, said the captain. Commissioned gunners have very loud voices. *Every man pick up a shell, follow your leader and strike down ammunition* roared the gunner, and they did. Unhappily the sailor who found himself in the lead was not at his best after an all-night journey from Chatham. Somehow he missed the ladder down to messdecks and magazines. Instead he galloped on and up to the fx'le. When he reached *Naiad's* bows he turned back towards the quarterdeck. In no time at all a couple of hundred sailors and stokers, each clutching an 80 lb shell, were doubling round the upper deck. This might have continued till total exhaustion intervened had not the near hysterical gunner joined the circling throng and found the correct hatchway to which he could direct the sweating, swearing mob.

Our guns and torpedoes unfired, our engines tried only slowly alongside the jetty, our ship's company largely untrained and ignorant of their duties, we waved our good byes and sailed to war.

CHAPTER 7

War at sea

Once more unto the breach, dear friends, once more
King Henry Vth William Shakespeare

MOST OFFICERS STANDING by *Naiad* while she was building in
1940 had experienced no wartime sea service. Those who joined
on our commissioning were mostly RNVR. Apart from the chief,
Commander (E) R W Marshall, who was one of the carefully
selected (E)s on the staff in my last Dartmouth term and the senior,
Lieutenant-Commander (E) Jock Finlay, there were no other ex-
Keyhams but we were blessed with two stalwart warrant engineers, Tom Browell, of vast experience and indomitable courage
and Jimmy Green, equally courageous, newly promoted and a
workaholic. There were also three uncertificated watchkeepers,
one from university and two from a scheme which was converting
junior shipyard engineers into temporary marine engineers. Captain
Marcel Kelsey was shyly agreeable. Commander Roy Dowling,
a charming tough Australian who was to rise to the top of his own
navy, was backed by the gunnery officer, Lieutenant-Commander
'Donc' Storey, another Australian with an irrepressible sense of
humour. This team from down under was completed by Warrant
Telegraphist Tregurtha. The torpedo officer, Lieutenant-Commander Dermot Gard, was quieter than his gunnery opposite
number, recently married, highly efficient and easy to get on with.
Lieutenant-Commander John Forbes was our navigator and, as
we were to discover, an able bomb dodger. The wardroom was

completed by a paymaster commander and a lieutenant commander RNR, a doctor, two splendid RNVR officers, 'Macgregor' Burns and John Holt and two other RN officers, Lieutenant J S Kerans, like me a member of the Dartmouth Drake Term, who was to make his post-war name with his astonishing dash down the Yangtse in *HMS Amethyst*, and the Sub, John Murray. Last, but certainly not least, was our splendidly named Royal Marine, Major Bullock. Besides Browell, Green and Tregurtha in the warrant officer's mess there were the gunner, Mr Balderton, the gunner (T) Mr Goldfinch, Mr Irish the chippie and Mr Maynard the signal boatswain.

Neither my chief nor senior was happy with the temporary (E) officers, willing though they were. Almost wholly inexperienced they found it difficult to establish rapport with the stokers or artificers. So Browell was made responsible for the engine rooms which he had nursed for several months and Green the boiler rooms in which he had been immured since joining. Because I had been to sea and was believed to understand the mysteries of damage control that became my parish, together with fuelling and the ship's watertightness.

After taking the machinery up to full power with some of Hawthorn Leslie's senior people on board we sped north firing our 5.25in High Angle/Low Angle guns at an aircraft-drawn drogue and in a throw-off shoot at a brave escorting destroyer. In Rosyth the captain formally accepted the ship from the builders who, after some stirrup cups, thankfully took train south. Soon after the admiral joined, bringing his flag lieutenant Jo Phillips, another of my Dartmouth term, and Commander Peter Pelly, staff officer plans. Of Rear-Admiral E L S King we lesser fry saw absolutely nothing, apart from one short visit to the wardroom. This we felt a pity and we continued deeply to regret our loss of the Mountbatten station-keeping gear.

From Rosyth we sailed to Scapa Flow, now with greatly improved anti-submarine, anti-aircraft and recreational arrangements, where we were inspected by the Admiral Commanding Orkneys and Shetlands, Vice Admiral T H Binney, my captain and mentor in the *Hood*. It was typical of him that he put aside a few moments for a chat with a very junior officer. After a quick work-up we were at sea from June 1940 to February 1941 virtually non-stop. The wardroom settled down happily and the temporary (E) officers received their watchkeeping certificates, albeit chief and senior keeping their fingers crossed. The senior was appointed away and I succeeded him which undoubtedly added another line to the chief's already furrowed brow. On my first day in this post I ran into crisis.

We had come to rest in Glasgow after weeks of near continuous seatime. Anticipating several days' stay there one watch of seamen and stokers was given leave until midnight by when only a few had returned; the remainder either insensible in pubs or in police cells. A 12-man patrol sent to round up the former returned shamefacedly about 0200 with only the petty officer, leading seaman and two young sailors and no leave breakers, the rest of the patrol having joined their mates in various drinking dens. My stokers were mainly Geordies whose predilection for fighting Scots had landed several in police hands, but a few came back as we received orders for a dawn sailing which we just managed despite thick heads and stokers enough to man only two watches. The guns' crews, in a similar dilemma, were also watch and watch which is hard work at any time, although fresh air revived them more quickly than did the heat and stink of the boiler rooms the stokers. The 'emergency' turned out to be a false alarm. Back in Glasgow a sorry crew were led on board by the police. A few who had been given leave the night before we never saw again, a loss we endured cheerfully. They were speedily replaced by a batch of inexperienced but eminently trainable young stokers and some young artificers which caused overcrowding. The artificers happily backed up some of their older brethren who were finding war routine physically tiring.

By now a reluctant engineer-in-chief had been persuaded to extend the period between boiler cleans to 750 hours from 21 days. Twenty-one days of 24 hours comes to a total of 504 hours but the rules had stated that a day was to be counted whenever the boiler had been steamed, if only for a few minutes. So the extension to 750 hours was even more welcome than it might seem. Operating continuously as we were, boiler cleaning was still an evolution to be carried out by all, however tired, after seatime in all weathers.

Three or four operations in the autumn and winter of 1940/41 stand out. *Naiad* was never to know the horrors of the Arctic convoys to Russia but as a result of Bletchley Park having decyphered signals indicating the date on which a weather station would be set up on Jan Mayen Island, we were ordered to destroy it and capture its scientists. By steaming fast through mountainous seas and drift ice and getting used to the huge icicles which appeared beneath the fan intakes in the normally sweltering boiler rooms, we just made it. *Naiad* arrived off Jan Mayen two hours before an enemy trawler appeared on which we trained our guns. She promptly ran aground hoping that if the scientists scrambled ashore we would not follow. Instead *Naiad* lowered her motor cutter with Kerans in command and the gunner, with an armed party and plenty of explosives in a whaler, towed astern. Kerans boarded the trawler and those Germans who escaped ashore were rounded up by the gunner and the whaler's crew who also set fire to the weather station. The vast cloud of smoke worried us all as either *Scharnhorst* or *Gneisenau* was rumoured to be in the vicinity.

Kerans returned to *Naiad* to offload his prisoners and then set off to collect the demolition party and remaining captives. As the swell increased things went wrong. Attempting to take off a load of chilled, wet men the whaler broached to in the icy surf and cast them all into the freezing shallows from which they struggled ashore. We were then treated to the sight of Germans and British doing physical jerks together under the stern commands of our gunner. Others, however, preferred to stand by the glowing ashes of the weather station. Sub Lieutenant John Murray was quickly dispatched in the remaining whaler to effect a rescue. In a remarkable display of seamanship he managed to get close enough for the party to wade out although he had some difficulty in coaxing the young Germans aboard. *Naiad's* homeward journey was through the worst weather we ever encountered and we were grateful that the ship had been so well put together. Nevertheless the four-inch steel pillars between the fx'le and main deck were permanently distorted as we crashed through mountainous seas. The rumoured proximity of *Scharnhorst* (or *Gneisenau*) undoubtedly had something to do with the speed achieved which was far too fast had good seamanship been the first consideration. Both Kerans and Murray received commendations for their efforts.

We spent Christmas day at sea in company with a battleship escorting a troop convoy. Having reached the prudent limit of our restricted range we were relieved by *HMS Berwick*. Soon after turning for home we heard that the convoy was under attack from the *Hipper* so we promptly reversed course. However, *Hipper*, not expecting to meet a battleship, had retired whereupon we set course for the Clyde, denouncing Mr De Valera and the Irish government as we did so for denying us bases nearer the south-west approaches.

After replenishing we were sent to Scapa Flow where we joined a sortie towards the southern tip of Norway, our purpose to protect merchantmen loaded with special steels and ball bearings breaking out from Gothenburg. This remarkable episode, masterminded by Mr (later Sir George) Binney and Captain Denham, the British naval attaché in Stockholm, succeeded and all five ships reached Kirkwall safely. On our way back we were attacked by German bombers, a severe assault we innocently thought. Later, when we returned to Newcastle to refit, Mr Fred Olsen, the merchant ships' owner gave us a most generous reception at the Station Hotel and announced that if after the war any of us would care to cruise in one of his ships he would be delighted to oblige. I dropped a hint to the firm 40 years later that my wife and I would be happy to accept the invitation, but sadly there was no reply.

At Dartmouth I recalled vividly Rear-Admiral (later Admiral Sir) William James, my first admiral in *Hood*, giving the College a talk entitled *The Golden Moment*. In it he suggested that certain admirals he named, throughout their lives had so seized what he called their 'copper' and 'silver' moments that they recognised their 'golden' moment when chance put it their way. He instanced that year's combined manoeuvres when a young lieutenant on the bridge of a cruiser had sighted smoke on the horizon. This, the admiral suggested, gave the young officer two options: he could turn his ship towards the smoke and order Full Speed or he could alert the captain and await orders. He chose the latter whereupon the enemy escaped. A moment had been missed.

It came back to me one clear dawn several hundred miles west of the Orkneys. Admiral King, in *Naiad*, with her sister ship *Phoebe*, were ahead of the Home Fleet with the commander-in-chief present in his flagship. Intelligence received suggested that *Scharnhorst* and *Gneisenau* would break out into the Atlantic to attack allied shipping. After securing from dawn action stations I had dallied in the engine room to discuss some problems with the chief artificer. Suddenly the revolution indicator from the bridge called for Full Speed and *Naiad* listed as the helm was put hard over. The boiler room telegraph was put to More Steam and then Full Speed, clearly an emergency. The turbine hum rose to a high pitched whine as the throttles were opened. Action Stations sounded and those who had just gone to breakfast came tumbling back into the machinery spaces. Kerans, the officer of the watch on the bridge, ever mindful of our lack of information down below, rang to say we had sighted the enemy.

We had reached about 75% full power when the revolution indicator clanged back to the original figure and the rudder indicator showed we were resuming course. Sizzling, because such treatment was good neither for machinery nor fuel consumption, I made my way to the bridge. A sharp-eyed boy lookout had spotted a puff of smoke on the horizon which was confirmed by Kerans, Storey (gunnery officer) and Forbes (navigator) who ordered the action described. By the time both admiral and captain reached the bridge there was no smoke to be seen so the former at once cancelled the chase. At that moment *Phoebe* reported that her rather primitive radar (with which *Naiad* was not yet fitted) revealed a couple of blips on the same bearing as the smoke. After a few lost minutes the c-in-c ordered *Naiad* to proceed at maximum speed towards the sighting. Below we did what we could; every sprayer was put onto each boiler, overspeed trips to the fans, supplying air to the furnaces, were gagged and we opened the by-pass valves to the later turbine stages to achieve maximum power. We worked up to a speed never since equalled by a British cruiser, in an eight-hour sustained dash with paravanes streamed, but to no avail. Eventually we returned to Scapa with our tail between our legs.

A subsequent enquiry decided we had gone off on a wild goose chase. No one was censured but those on the bridge were deemed to have acted precipitately. When the German archives were opened after the war it was discovered that *Naiad* had sighted *Scharnhorst* and *Gneisenau* under Admiral Lutjens. The more effective German radar had enabled them to spot our force and turn away at full speed (which caused the puff of smoke seen by the boy seaman). They detoured around and behind the British battle fleet and so broke out to the Atlantic, the very act we were there to prevent. Had the small group on the bridge been permitted to seize their Golden Moment *Naiad* and the slower battleships may not have caught up the German ships but just might have prevented their embarking on the two-month foray which cost the allies 120,000 tons of shipping and god knows how many lives. Returning to Brest Lutjens was sighted by *Ark Royal* aircraft, but the weather closed in and both his ships reached France safely. Luck was certainly with him.

Naiad's next operation might have turned to tragedy. *HMS King George V* had to be escorted from the Tyne to Rosyth so that her two outer propellers could be fitted in dock. As the Germans might try to prevent this transfer *Naiad* was sent to the Tyne with a dozen destroyers to escort the battleship. The operation was kept so secret that *Naiad* and her force, proceeding by night down the swept channel at 20 knots, unexpectedly met another speeding cruiser northbound. Happily both ships got challenge and reply correct,but both were towards the centre of the mine-free channel and only yards separated them as they passed each other at 50 mph. A thick fog descended at dawn and one of the destroyers, sent ahead on an anti-submarine search, mistook a buoy off the Tyne entrance and finished up on South Shields beach where she caught fire, to the surprise of soldiers stationed there and the hastily summoned fire brigade. When the fog lifted *King George V* emerged with the destroyer escort, a flying boat above and a combat air patrol somewhere above that. With *Naiad* on the port quarter we quietly proceeded northwards, tension easing. At this moment an enthusiastic petty officer on the starboard torpedo tubes (always trained on the beam at sea) told a newly-joined torpedoman, *and to fire it you pull this lever,* suiting the action to his words. Everything worked perfectly. The torpedo's track could be seen streaking just astern of *King George V*. *Naiad's* radio broadcast of her mistake was barely in time to prevent a depth charge attack by air and sea. Dermot Gard, the torpedo officer, hid his head.

By February 1941 *Naiad* had had eight months non-stop running; the pillars beneath the fx'le were still bent, teething troubles were mounting and we required docking. Hawthorn Leslies were too busy to take us but Palmer's yard, just down the road, had a free berth and a dock for the next three or four frenzied weeks. As usual defect rectification revealed other problems but eventually we were ready for a basin trial when the main engines could be moved slowly. A severe leak at a main steam line joint appeared. Its repair meant so much dismantling that shore power would be needed. In pre-war designs the engineer-in-chief, unlike his opposite numbers in the French and German navies, so distrusted diesel generators that few if any were fitted. As our berth was required for a damaged destroyer we were towed across the river to the Tyne Commissioner's Quay adjoining a huge timber yard where power was available and extra fitters could be ferried across to help. Most of our ship's company went on leave, blessing the engineers who had to stay behind with a few unlucky sailors to man the pom-poms and machine guns, the only armament available in the event of an air-raid. When work on the steam line was complete and we were raising steam the luftwaffe staged a major raid on Newcastle. Early on a shower of incendiaries set alight the timber yard so that when the next wave of bombers arrived *Naiad* was silhouetted starkly against the flames. Both the captain and Dick Marshall, my chief, were on leave, so the commander, the indomitable warrant engineer, Tom Browell and one or two other officers including myself were left holding the fort. I was on the bridge telling the commander we were raising steam as fast as we dared with newly-made joints when the shore power failed as a wave of bombers arrived. It seemed prudent to seek protection below, although our fairly thin deck plating was unlikely to offer much resistance. At that moment my Guardian Angel took over: a stick of bombs fell alongside and blew me off the bridge ladder. It also rendered me temporarily deaf in one ear and gave me the tinnitus, a perpetual and sometimes infuriating noise in the head, which I still have. The next stick fell even closer, splintering the ladder from which I had been blown and literally bouncing the ship.

Bemused, I went down to comfort the artificers and stokers waiting apprehensively in the gloom of emergency lighting for enough steam to start a dynamo and give us some power. So great had been the bounce that we assumed the ship was seriously damaged although we were not listing. There had been no panic but my battered appearance elicited some leg-pulling about the dangers of deserting my post below for the bridge. When lighting was restored and we could examine the machinery we found the cast iron 'keeps' holding down the turbine feet had fractured. From a cruiser with no steam and good main engines we became a cruiser with plenty of steam but no engines.

Next day *Naiad* was towed ignominiously to a wharf in the middle of the city where, the authorities decided, we could usefully provide anti-aircraft protection for the adjoining road and rail bridges. It would take about a week to fabricate new steel turbine feet 'keeps', far less liable to fracture should we suffer any more near misses. We lay but a few minutes' walk from the Eldon and rather less from the Turk's Head so all our old cronies, who assumed that *Naiad's* wardroom, like the Windmill Theatre, never closed tottered on board whenever their favourite hostelries shut for the night. We were as glad to see them as Newcastle Breweries were to keep us supplied, but all good things come to an end. Our friends joined us for one last, happily air-raid free evening to celebrate Cunningham's victory at Matapan and bid us farewell. Before casting off next morning, the crew of a recently refitted pom-pom decided to emulate the torpedoman who had had a shot at the *King George V* and inadvertently opened fire across the river. *Naiad's* luck held again and, although the warehouse on the opposite bank looked less rain-tight after receiving an unexpected volley, there were no casualties. Clearly it was time to go to war again.

• *HMS Naiad in Scapa in her new camouflage*

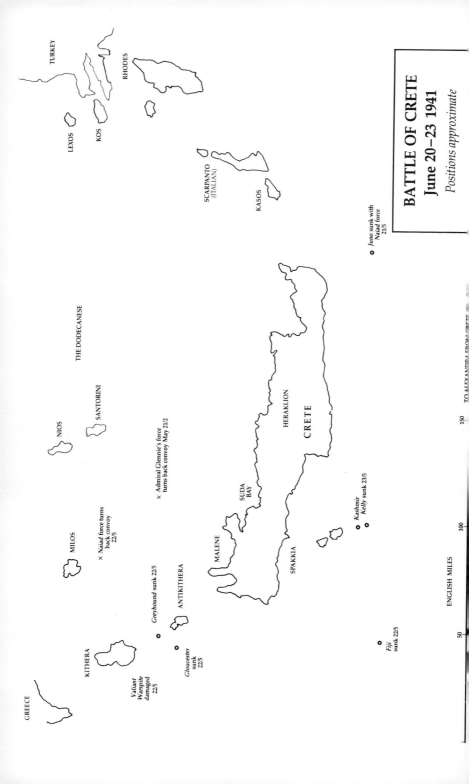

GREECE

KITHERA

Valiant
Warspite damaged
22/5

Gloucester
sunk 22/5

ANTIKITHERA

Greyhound sunk 22/5

MILOS

× *Naiad* force turns
back convoy 22/5

NIOS

SANTORINI

× Admiral Glennie's force
turns back convoy May 21/2

THE DODECANESE

MALENE

SUDA
BAY

HERAKLION

CRETE

SPAKKIA

Kashmir
Kelly sunk 23/5

Fiji
sunk 22/5

LEXOS

KOS

RHODES

TURKEY

SCARPANTO
(ITALIAN)

KASOS

Juno sunk with
Naiad force
21/5

BATTLE OF CRETE
June 20–23 1941
Positions approximate

TO ALEXANDRA FROM CRETE

50   100   150

ENGLISH MILES

CHAPTER 8

In the Mediterranean

Stick it out. Navy must not let Army down. No enemy forces must reach Crete by sea.
C-in-C to Mediterranean fleet, May 22, 1941

THE NIGHT BEFORE OUR departure we learned that the *Bonaventure*, a sister ship whose officers we knew well, had been sunk in the Mediterranean. Cunningham, I was told, was perturbed that one torpedo could so quickly send a new cruiser to the bottom. I explained that the *Dido* class to which *Naiad* and *Bonaventure* belonged, with five turrets and in a low oil condition, could be unstable. The director of naval construction and the engineer-in-chief forbade our admitting water either to watertight compartments or to empty fuel tanks which would have brought down the centre of gravity and thus compensate for lack of fuel, a condition exacerbated if much ammunition had been expended. Representations from sea about this design failure had been made, to which I suggested our admiral might add his voice. I never heard that he did.

During our refit in 1941 we had acquired radar and a delightful young Canadian sub-lieutenant to act as its high priest. We also gained an ordnance engineer officer, Lieutenant-Commander (E) Masters who, surprisingly, was given the (executive) duties of fighter direction officer as well as technical responsibility for our main and secondary armament. Materially we were in much better shape and this, combined with our eight months' 'running in', gave us confidence in our ship as an effective fighting weapon. We were to need it all.

We moved north to the Clyde where a large troop convoy was assembling. The messdeck buzz was that we were going round the Cape to the eastern Mediterranean. While we waited in Loch Striven *Naiad* was invited to remove a bomb which had lodged in the hold of a merchant ship. A valiant bomb disposal officer assured my artificer welder and me that he had removed the fuze and he thought it would be OK to weld on an eyebolt by the tail. Happily it was. We embarked a contingent of soldiers who made the messdecks and wardroom insufferably crowded, but they were a patient lot, mostly Gunners, with a sprinkling of Northumberland Fusiliers. The escort included *HMS Queen Elizabeth* and *HMS Fiji*, a heavier cruiser than ourselves. Some destroyers and *Naiad* were detached to Gibraltar to fuel which meant hiding the soldiers, allowing them on deck only in dribs and drabs and dressed as sailors which caused much hilarity. After fuelling we headed *westwards* along the Spanish shore, confident that our course would be reported, and then, when darkness fell, turned back. By dawn next day, May 7, 1941, now well to the *east*, we met up with *Ark Royal, Renown, Malaya, Sheffield* and *Gloucester*, part of Admiral Somerville's Force H, which considerably strengthened the escort. On May 8 we had our first real taste of bombing: *Ark Royal's* fighters and our combined firepower destroyed seven bombers for no hits on the convoy or escort. That night as we approached the Sicilian Narrows two of the convoy struck mines and one, *Empire Song*, sank. *New Zealand Star*, the other victim, managed to carry on. Next day we met our old friends *Dido* and *Phoebe*, as well as *Carlisle, Calcutta* and *Coventry* and the rest of Admiral Cunningham's Mediterranean fleet in support but out of sight; while Force H turned west to Gibraltar. Providence now took a hand: a thick mist enveloped us until we had passed Malta, an unusual and welcome phenomenon for that time of year.

Such luck could not last. With 48 hours to go, a flat sea and a full moon, an air attack developed heavier than anything *Naiad* had experienced. My night in the engine room was heartened by the presence of Commander (later Admiral Sir) Dymock Watson. Wattie had been a feature of *Hood's* wardroom as a lieutenant-commander, chairman of our 'wheeler's club', a team of bicycle enthusiasts who would explore the hinterland during peacetime visits to Mediterranean ports. He was taking passage to become Cunningham's fleet torpedo officer.

I shall never have the chance of learning what it's like to be in an engine room in action, he explained, *so I might as well try it now.*

Despite heavy bombing we reached Alexandria safely and delivered the contents of the four surviving merchant ships of Operation Tiger to the Army. The operation's background is worth an explanation.

While we were restoring *Naiad* to a battleworthy condition in Newcastle momentous war decisions were being taken in London and the Middle East. General Wavell had cleared Cyrenaica of Italian forces and was similarly engaged in Somaliland and Ethiopia. His North African success had exhausted his army who had lost most of their tanks in battle, the remainder now unserviceable. The famous Seventh Armoured Division which had spearheaded Wavell's advance to El Agheila, the sea/land hinge between Cyrenaica and Tripolitania, had been withdrawn to Cairo. Meanwhile the decision had been taken to support Greece against first, the Italian attack and, more serious, the later German advance through Hungary and Yugoslavia.

El Agheila was held by comparatively light forces, and the navy had been greatly stretched bringing up petrol and supplies to Benghazi whose harbour needed to be restored to working order. Mersa Matruh, Tobruk and Derna, also, had to be kept supplied during which the naval inshore squadron suffered heavy losses. On top of it all Malta had to be reinforced with two infantry battalions from Alexandria.

The Greek campaign put another burden on the navy. From March 5 onwards every ship not otherwise occupied on the North African coast was engaged in escorting convoys, or in ferrying a British armoured brigade, three Australian and New Zealand divisions, and a Polish brigade, with much of the remaining desert army impedimenta from North Africa to Greece. Supplies for the attenuated, hard-pressed RAF also required shipping. Only a month later, with the army not yet deployed and the RAF lacking sufficient airfields, the Germans invaded both Greece and Yugoslavia, simultaneously launching a massive air raid on Piraeus. A lucky hit on an ammunition ship not only destroyed the port but also sank 11 merchant ships, including several yet to be unloaded.

Our victory at Matapan, which we had so lightheartedly celebrated on our last night in Newcastle, kept the Italian fleet out of the struggle for the Aegean, but air attack from Rhodes meant that every ship leaving Egypt for Greece now had to run the gauntlet.   When Yugoslavia collapsed the full might of the German armies was directed against the Greek, British and Imperial forces taking position.   By mid-April, as *Naiad* was reaching the Clyde, Greece was collapsing.   Once again the navy had to evacuate our outnumbered army and air force, as well as the Greek government and royal family.   As at Dunkirk most heavy equipment had to be abandoned.   The New Zealanders and some Australians were taken to Crete, clearly the next German target.   Others were returned to Egypt where disaster loomed.   On April 24 Cunningham had to signal, *the object is to embark men, if possible with arms; but no material must be allowed to take precedence to men.   Troopships with men embarked to sail direct to Alexandria, except* Glen *ships which must unload at Suda Bay and do a second embarkation.   Destroyers to take their troops to Crete, where they will be transferred later.*

Our incursion into Greece had been based on the army's ability to hold El Agheila and eventually build up sufficient forces to move into Tripolitania but two other events intervened.   In mid-February Rommel took command of the German, and subsequently the Italian, North African forces;   secondly massive air attacks on Malta prevented our bombing Tripoli, the focus of the main German/Italian supply line, thus allowing considerable nazi forces to be brought across to form the Afrika Corps.   At the height of the Greek crisis Rommel attacked and took El Agheila.   By April 7 Benghazi had fallen and, a few days later,   Tobruk itself was invested.

In mid-April Churchill drafted one of his more infuriating (in the circumstances, ridiculous) directives laying upon the Royal Navy their prime task (to him) of preventing seaborne reinforcements reaching Tripoli.   That port should be continually bombed and, if possible, bombarded from the sea.   The harbour's entrance was to be blocked by the sinking of a battleship, *HMS Barham*.   The Mediterranean fleet was to be reinforced to carry out these demands, easier to write than to carry out.   Churchill failed to comprehend the navy's essential tasks: the army's evacuation from Greece, the attempted seizure of Rhodes,   supplying the Tobruk garrison and the clearance of the Suez canal now endangered by German acoustic and magnetic mines.

In April 1941 Wavell told Churchill of the situation resulting from Rommel's thrust to the Egyptian frontier leaving Tobruk with its British garrison now in his rear. Wavell further reported that if as feared another German armoured division had arrived Rommel would possess an even greater preponderance of armour over Wavell's after the Greek and El Agheila disasters. Churchill at once returned to a scheme which the chiefs of staff had resisted. On April 20 he persuaded them that part of convoy WS 7, carrying tanks for Egypt via the Cape, should be diverted through the Mediterranean and 48 hours later arrangements had been so made. *Naiad* sailed with the convoy on April 23 and, as described earlier, Operation Tiger entered the Mediterranean shortly afterwards, another responsibility for Cunningham. Somehow he fulfilled all the tasks, except the sinking of *Barham* in Tripoli harbour which he judged unlikely to succeed, would entail the sacrifice of most of her ship's company and the confidence of the fleet. So, for the loss of one merchant ship, *Naiad* and the rest of the Tiger escort under the umbrella first of Force H and then of the eastern Mediterranean fleet, managed to deliver 235 of the 295 tanks originally confided to us. In the haste with which the tanks had been loaded, the air filters, so essential in desert sand and dust, had been omitted. A similar oversight grounded the 43 Hurricanes which had just arrived. As Cunningham morosely wrote to the first sea lord, *So there, under one roof, 100 yards from* Warspite *at this moment, about 100 of these valuable tanks are collected and will be there for about 14 days or longer with German aircraft flying around every night. Why on earth these filters aren't fitted before they are shipped I can't think. The 43 Hurricanes are just the same congregated on a nearby aerodrome having filters fitted.*

By now Alexandria harbour was crowded with Admiral Godfroy's immobilised French squadron and our own ships. I had a bevy of cousins in Alexandria whose invitations made me free of their homes at any time, but there was too much to do on board. With the evacuation of Greece ending and the need to reinforce Crete, we had to tear into boiler cleaning, change evaporator coils and make good the usual minor defects. Captain Berthon, my erstwhile chief in *Hood* and now port engineer officer with all the port facilities including repair ships at his disposal, gave us particularly useful advice.

Make sure of your steering gear, that everyone knows what should be done if the primary steering system fails; but above all try and ensure it never fails. Bomb dodging is an art your captain and navigator, if they are lucky, will quickly learn. To be successful, instantaneous reaction to speed orders from the bridge and a reliable steering gear are essential.

Berthon's brother had been killed after commanding a destroyer at Dunkirk so the destroyers and smaller ships in Alexandria were his particular care. He would board them from his motor boat at whatever hour they entered harbour and, then, having surveyed the damage and listed their problems and defects, he gave all the unstinting help that his organisation could provide.

Everyone assumed that Crete was to be the next big battle. And so we worked hard, each to his task, preparing for an ordeal which we guessed would try us and *Naiad* to the very limit.

Hardly had *Naiad* come to her buoy in Alexandria early on May 12 than my chief was told we had barely 72 hours to bring all the machinery to immediate readiness. After 19 days' of watchkeeping and several severe bombing attacks this struck us as a bit hard: we had not appreciated the Mediterranean pace to which we would have to conform. A run ashore for the most hardworked artificers and stokers had just been organised when orders came to raise steam for our first operation. By May 16 we were in position north of Crete with two other groups of light forces.

By then the bombing of Maleme and Heraklion airfields had started and we could guess at the soldiers' ordeal as we swept along Crete's northern coast. The German assault seemed to be delayed while the softening up process went on, so we returned to Alexandria to top up with fuel. By May 20 we were back in the Aegean furnace. Our task, the captain explained, with two other groups, one of them under Rear-Admiral Glennie who had been my captain in *Hood*, was to prevent enemy forces from reaching Crete by sea. To accomplish this would mean spending many daylight hours with little RAF fighter support within range of German airfields in Greece and Rhodes.

History now records that in the first three or four days some 24,000 German troops were to arrive in Crete. Besides 500 troop-carrying aircraft with towed gliders there were more than 800 torpedo and dive bombers, fighters and reconnaissance aircraft under General Von Richthoven, a cousin of the world war one ace. The airborne attack started early on May 20. As we fought off dive-bombing attacks we saw Junkers 82s towing gliders and disgorging parachute troops onto the Cretan airfields. That night we swept inshore to assist the army but, though we could see the fighting, we were unable to distinguish German troops from ours so there was no chance of intervening. So close were we that the scent of wild garlic permeated even the boiler rooms. To this day that unmistakable smell recalls those hectic hours.

We engaged six Italian motor torpedo boats and sank or damaged four. As dawn came we withdrew to the southward. High level bombing attacks pursued us and while on deck I saw *Juno*, one of our destroyer escorts, receive a bomb in her magazine which sank her almost immediately. During the night of May 21/22 Admiral Glennie with *Dido, Orion, Ajax* and four destroyers met an Italian escorted convoy. Within two hours the transports were sunk and some 2500 German seaborne reinforcements left to drown or swim ashore, with no British casualties. Glennie was lucky. The darkness, during which the Germans had hoped to sneak in reinforcements by sea, was the navy's ally. The Germans quickly realised our night-fighting skills and swopped tactics. They dispatched the next large convoy by day, to become *Naiad's* target on May 22.

Admiral King's force consisted of *Naiad, Calcutta, Carlisle*, the Australian cruiser *Perth* and three destroyers. It should have been joined by Admiral Glennie's force but he had had to return to

• *A painting by E Tufnell of Naiad under attack at about 10.30, see deck log extract at end of chapter (Crown Copyright)*

Alexandria almost out of ammunition. On May 21 the German airforce had concentrated on the land battle. Next day the Mediterranean fleet was their main target. As the log at the end of this chapter reveals the attack on *Naiad* and the rest of the squadron started at dawn and continued for 15 hours. At 0830 a caique full of German soldiers was sighted and sunk as was another small troopship an hour later. We then sighted a collection of caiques and small merchant vessels escorted by a destroyer and a motor torpedo boat. The destroyer managed to lay a smoke screen and escape but the other escort and several caiques were sunk, while the convoy was forced back to Milos.

By 1100 we had been in action for five and a half hours against high level, dive and torpedo bombers. Our decks had been machine-gunned with phosphorus-tipped bullets inflicting terrible wounds on our short range weapon's crews and setting some of the ready-use ammunition alight. Our high angle (anti-aircraft) director tower had been hit and Sub-Lieutenant Page, the splendid young Canadian, mortally wounded. Major Bullock lost an eye and there were numerous casualties, several fatal, above and below decks. Then a near-miss blew in our starboard side for'd well below the waterline and flooded the small arms magazine. The resultant inrush of water, for we were at full-speed, burst open the hatch to the messdeck above. The water taken in there brought *Naiad* down for'd and more water started to pour through the splinter holes (400 were later counted) in the ship's side, holes which the damage control parties had not yet had time to plug. A large messdeck was in danger of filling up and I was sent to help Mr Irish the shipwright shore down the hatch through which water continued to gush. So with the survivors of the local damage control party, sometimes up to our necks as the ship heeled under full helm to avoid the next stick of bombs, we wrestled to stem the flooding. Not the least of our difficulties were the mangled bodies of those killed by splinters and the clothing from broken kit lockers which blocked the suction hoses lowering the water level. In the end we had to ask the bridge to slow down for a few moments: no sooner had the squadron's speed eased than *Carlisle* was hit.

By now X turret (aft) had used up its ammunition and A magazine (for'd) still with some left but the turret itself temporarily out of action was flooding up through a damaged bulkhead from the adjacent small arms magazine, wide open to the sea. So the magazine crew, already up to their knees in the rising water and in semi-darkness lit only by secondary lighting, had to pass ammunition manually from the magazine, along the messdecks and then down into the empty X turret whose guns remained serviceable. Air attacks came from every angle but we were lucky: one air-launched torpedo passed harmlessly under our stern. Later, after docking, we found that another had punched a hole through our stem without exploding.

When the German troop convoy turned back, Admiral King, aware that his squadron's ammunition supply was practically exhausted, retired towards *Fiji* and *Gloucester* who had been sent to support us. Tragedy almost immediately ensued. The destroyer *Greyhound* was sunk by a salvo of bombs. *Kingston* and *Kandahar* went to pick up survivors and Admiral King, the senior officer in the battle area, sent *Fiji* and *Gloucester* to give them cover. With hindsight this was a mistake. The admiral was unaware that both cruisers were also desperately short of ammunition. Quickly the gallant *Gloucester* was hit by a salvo of bombs which sank her. *Fiji*, by now down to firing her practice ammunition, correctly left her and dropped all her Carley floats to help *Gloucester*'s swimmers in the water.

The situation was desperate and a brave and determined Admiral Rawlings, commanding the battle fleet, brought it into the Kithera Channel to support the cruisers, but the cost was heavy and *Warspite* and *Valiant* were both damaged. Next *Fiji* was attacked by a single plane and an unlucky hit blew in her side abreast the engine room. Then another aircraft scored a further hit and *Fiji* rolled over and sank. Unlike *Gloucester* however, whose survivors were machine-gunned and mostly killed in the water, many of *Fiji*'s ship's company, even without their Carley floats, were picked up after dark by *Kingston* and *Kandahar*.

On May 22 Admiral Cunningham made the signal quoted at the beginning of this chapter, but the price of preventing seaborne forces reaching Crete had not yet been fully paid. That night, our old friend from Newcastle days, HMS *Kelly*, with Mountbatten in command, together with *Kashmir* and *Kipling*, was sent to intercept more seaborne troops trying to filter onto northern Crete. After sinking two caiques full of soldiers and bombarding the German-held Maleme airfield onto which troop-carrying aircraft were still landing, the small force turned for Alexandria at full-speed. At about 0830 they were attacked by a posse of 24 dive bombers and *Kashmir* was sunk almost at once. *Kelly*, at 30 knots and under full helm, was hit by another stick of bombs and turned turtle. Her commander (E) and those of the engine room crew still alive, found themselves in an air-lock, so fast had *Kelly* turned over. Several contrived to swim down through the engine room hatch and so to the surface. Many of *Kashmir's* and *Kelly's* people had been killed in the original bombing; many more were machine-gunned in the oily water. Courageously *Kipling*, despite three hours of intensive attack, rescued a large number of survivors, including Captain Mountbatten.

During a prolonged bombing attack such as we endured, engine and boiler rooms resemble the inside of a giant's kettle against which a sledge-hammer is being beaten with uncertain aim. Sometimes there was an almighty clang; sometimes the giant, in his frustration, seemed to pick up the kettle and shake and even kick it. The officer detailed to broadcast a running commentary suffered a breakdown during the battle so we heard little below, but through the noise and heat of the machinery spaces we came to understand something of what was happening on deck. Suddenly more speed would be called for, then we would hear our 5.25in turrets opening fire which told us aircraft were attacking. Next the bridge telegraphs might move to Emergency Full Speed and we would see the rudder indicator go to hard-a-port or starboard at the moment of bomb release. This would be followed by the sound of *Naiad's* short-range weapons as the bomber pulled out of its dive or the torpedo bomber dropped its torpedo. We learned to interpret, by the ensuing shake or shudder or clang, the success or otherwise of our navigator's avoiding action. Occasionally the damage control officer would ring me with reports of damage received or casualties suffered; occasionally my valiant chief stoker would report the fuel expenditure and his plans to keep the boilers supplied as our fuel reserves dwindled or seawater contamination from near-misses adjacent to some tanks showed up in his scrupulous testing.

From time to time my chief or I would visit the boiler rooms. Here, for hour after frightening hour, with ears popping from the air pressure, the young stokers knew and heard little of what was going on apart from the obvious near-misses and the scream of the boiler room fans. On their alertness, as they watched for orders to open or shut off oil sprayers to the furnaces, depended the precise supply of steam available to meet the sudden changes of speed ordered from the bridge, on which *Naiad's* survival depended. The more imaginative amongst them, no doubt, tried not to think which would be worse, to be boiled by superheated steam, cremated or drowned. Commander Marshall and I, in our respective engine rooms, spoke often by phone and when not visiting the boiler rooms one or other would go round the damage control parties and tell the bridge of the situation down below.

If I have been critical of the engineer-in-chief's department for the lack of peacetime advance in machinery design, it must be said that what we had, agricultural though some of it may have seemed compared to land practice, stood up to battle-pounding admirably. Had Winkle and his engineering friends at Hawthorn Leslie's yard not done their work so well or had those who operated the machinery failed to keep their nerve and watch over each machine or gauge, we should not have survived.

One irreparable loss was Chief Stoker Whittle, the regulating chief stoker I had selected on my first day as senior engineer. The next six months, in the general air of stability on the stoker's messdecks, confirmed the wisdom of my choice and now he was gone, killed towards the end of the action by a stray splinter as he went about his other task of ensuring the continuity of our fuel supply. He fought for his life for many hours, but when I went aft at night to see him buried with a shell at his feet, the commander broke the near unbelievable news that *Hood* had blown up. That there was another world outside the conflict in which we were engaged was difficult enough to comprehend, that the navy should be fighting two such great sea battles, so many thousand miles apart, was almost beyond understanding; but that the ship in which I had been weaned and I had come to love should have disappeared in seconds was a kick in the stomach.

It was hot and sultry in Alexandria harbour when *Naiad*, well down by the bows, limped in and secured to a buoy as, overhead, a German reconnaissance aircraft flew high above the black puffs of bursting shells from optimistic Egyptian aircraft batteries. No doubt the observer could see the masses of shipping in the harbour but he could hardly have distinguished the two large hospital barges which secured on either side of *Naiad*; nor could he have seen the torn bodies lying white-faced on their stretchers or heard the half-stifled groan or tight-lipped jest as they were manoeuvred down the narrow gangway. Nor could he have heard anything from the other barge for, from the dead, lying at last in peace, there could come no sound.

As the last of the wounded were carried down the gangway, we mustered on the quarterdeck looking so much more careworn than on commissioning day, eleven months before. After a service in remembrance of those taken away by the barges and those buried at sea we gave thanks for our own deliverance. Our drawn and rather haggard captain, his arm in a sling, spoke to us of the gun's crews who had fought their guns till they dropped, of the magazine crew who had worked in the dark in a rising flood of water, of the signal boy who had twice swarmed aloft and re-rigged wireless aerials twice shot away and of the Royal Marine who had ditched the burning ammunition from a ready use locker.

There was a moment, he said, *when, due to casualties and damage Stukas dived on us unopposed; no guns were firing. We are here because when I asked for Full Speed, I got more than full speed; and when I caused the wheel to be put over, we turned like a taxicab in a London street. Indeed I would say that, occasionally, during last Thursday, we on the upper deck had moments when we could pause and take stock. But if, for a moment throughout that long action, the engines had faltered or the steering had not functioned, we should now be with those friends we have left lying beneath the sea around Crete.*

It was heartwarming particularly when my chief was asked to submit a list for awards. Quite rightly young Ordnance Artificer Bache, who had so inspired the crew of the flooding magazine, received the Distinguished Service Medal, but the only other acknowledgement was a mention in despatches for the chief cook whose welcome bully beef sandwiches had vanished in such quantities. No one seeks awards but Marshall was as disappointed as I was that some of the efforts of those down below, particularly old Leading Stoker Lambkin in his steering gear compartment, immured beneath three inches of armour which could be opened only from above, and four thundering propellers his only companions, had not been recognised.

When our army in Crete could fight no more the Mediterranean fleet, now reduced from four battleships, a carrier, 12 cruisers and 30 destroyers to less than a quarter of that number, had to remove from the rugged southern Cretan shore whatever soldiers were left, in the face of overwhelming air attack.

Just as Cunningham began to believe there were no more evacuation tasks for his battered ships, a personal appeal from

New Zealand's prime minister then in Egypt, triggered one final desperate operation. The fleet's last serviceable squadron, *Phoebe*, *Abdiel*, *Hotspur*, *Jackal* and *Kimberley* was sent to bring off the brave New Zealanders who had fought their way across Crete to Spakhia. Amazingly the squadron suffered no loss, but *Calcutta*, with her brilliant fighting record was bombed and sunk after being sent out from Alexandria to help fight off air attacks against the other ships so heavily laden with soldiers. Despite the New Zealand government's recent apparent pacifist stance, I hope some there will recall the bravery of their fighting men (a cousin of mine amongst them), as well as the sacrifices the Royal Navy made to help them out of the desperate situation into which their immense loyalty to the Old Country had brought them.

Except for those of us who had to remain to keep the coal-fired dock boilers alight to maintain steam to work the pumps (the Arab stokers having sensibly fled) most of *Naiad's* crew were sent ashore until a parachute mine, lodged under the floating dock in which we lay, had been defused. Thereafter, with the help of the repair ships, we set about welding a great plate over the huge hole for'd and repairing the multitude of splinter holes and other damage. Many of the sailors, led by Kerans, were helping to restore *Orion* and at the same time remove the remains of the 300 soldiers killed when a bomb penetrated a crowded messdeck during her last trip from Crete. On the few opportunities to get ashore my cousins' ever-open bar was much appreciated. Then, unexpectedly, the French turned on us in Syria and *Naiad* was needed quickly on the Lebanese coast. So, our repairs more or less completed, some though not all of the essential replacements for our casualties hastily sent on board, we undocked, re-ammunitioned, re-fuelled and steamed at full speed to Haifa.

HMS NAIAD - THURSDAY 22 MAY, 1941
Extract from Deck Log in Public Record Office

0539	2 aircraft bearing 040. *Naiad* opened fire.
0602	Aircraft bearing 220 left in westerly direction.
0622	1 Dornier 215 crossing bow of *Naiad*.
0636	*Naiad* sighted 1 Dornier 215 reconnaissance plane.
0655	1 float plane 000.
0732	*Perth* opened fire on 1 Ju 88 on starboard bow.
0815	3 aircraft crossing *Naiad's* bows port to starboard.
0820	1 aircraft on port bow of *Naiad*.
0821	*Naiad* opened fire.
0821½	7 bombs dropped astern of *Kandahar*.
0825	4 bombs dropped 5 cables on starboard beam of *Naiad*.
0832	Caique No 5 painted green, full of troops and stores flying swastika flag, sighted by *Naiad*.
0834	*Naiad* after group opened fire on caique - not sunk.
0835	Stick of bombs astern of *Carlisle*.
0840	4 bombs port side of *Calcutta*.
0844	8 bombs near *Perth*.
0846	Aircraft damaged by pom-poms of *Naiad*.
0850	Caique on fire, boat pulling away.
0900	Caique sinking, *Perth* rejoining.
0901	Caique sunk.
0902	3 torpedo bombers attacking *Calcutta*. *Carlisle* and destroyers.
0903	3 more torpedo bombers attacking *Calcutta*, *Carlisle* and destroyers.
	14 torpedo bombers in all counted.
0905	*Calcutta* reports some of torpedo bombers were transports heading south.
0912	*Naiad* opened fire on aircraft passing astern
0916	Near miss port side of *Perth*.
0919	Bomb starboard side of *Perth*.
0923	Near miss by dive bombers on port quarter of *Perth*.
	Aircraft damaged losing height rapidly.
0927	Near miss by dive bombers on port quarter of *Perth*.
0928	Near miss astern of *Perth*.
0930	2 bombs well astern of *Perth*.
0932	Ju 88 dropped 3 bombs astern of *Nubian*.
0934	1 bomb dropped off port quarter of *Naiad*.
0937	4 bombs astern of *Perth*.
0939	2 bombs dropped astern of two destroyers.
0941	2 bombs astern of *Perth*.
0945	4 bombs dropped astern of *Kandahar*.
0947	3 bombs off port quarter of *Naiad*.
0948	2 bombs dropped 2 cables on port bow of *Naiad*.
0950	1 bomb 50 yards fine on port bow of *Naiad*.
0950½	1 dud in wake of *Naiad*.
0954	1 bomb 100 yards off port quarter of *Naiad*.
0957	2 bombs off starboard bow of *Perth*.
1001	2 bombs short on starboard side of *Naiad*.
	Passed Caique and six small boats flying white flag.
1007	8 small bombs in wake of *Naiad*.
1010	1 enemy destroyer (Italian) bearing 330, course 220 - 24 knots covering 6 sailing caiques.
1012	1 small bomb dropped ahead of *Naiad*.
	1 big bomb astern of *Naiad*.
	Destroyer being engaged, shells port and starboard bow, one shell ahead.
1014	Enemy straddled.
	4 bombs in wake of *Naiad*.
1015	Destroyer making smoke. Aircraft continuously attacking.
1017	6 bombs off port quarter. Destroyer disengaged.
1021	2 bombs in wake of *Naiad*.
1024	Delayed action bomb off port beam of *Naiad*.
1027	2 bombs starboard bow very close (50 yards) off *Naiad*.
1028	11 bombs (1 stick) and 3 others 1 cable starboard side of *Naiad*.
1030	6 bombs in wake of *Naiad*.
1032	5 bombs starboard quarter of *Naiad*.

1034	2 large bombs close port quarter of *Naiad*.
1035	2 bombs 40 yards starboard beam of *Naiad*.
1036	6 bombs (3 close starboard quarter of *Naiad*).
1037	2 bombs 500 yards astern of *Naiad*.
1040	3 bombs port side (1 near miss, 1 casualty in after tower of *Naiad*.)
1041	2 bombs starboard quarter of *Naiad*.
1044	Milo Peak bearing 022.
1046	2 bombs 4 cables port beam of *Naiad*.
1053	Sailing caique bearing 184.
1056	1 unknown vessel bearing 200 making lot of smoke.
1056	3 aircraft bearing 280.
1058	2 bombs 60 yards off port bow of *Naiad*.
1102	5 bombs 60 yards off port bow of *Naiad*.
1103	10 troop carriers on port bow of *Naiad*.
1105	9 bombs on port quarter (on line 60° to M.L.A.) of *Naiad*.
1107	1 bomb near *Naiad*.
1110	13 bombs astern of *Naiad*.
1112	3 bombs starboard beam of *Naiad*.
	3 bombs port bow of *Naiad*.
1112	500-ton steamer bearing 200.
1114	1 stick (6 heavy bombs) off starbord quarter of *Naiad*.
1115	2 sticks (3 aircraft) starboard side of *Naiad*.
1116	Near miss port side, near miss starboard side of *Naiad*.
1117	*Naiad* attacked by 3 torpedo bombers.
1120	2 bombs starboard quarter of*Naiad*.
	H.A.D.T. out of action.
	After tower in action again.
	Small arms magazine flooding.
1122	X turret ammunition expended.
1123	2 formations of 5 aircraft on starboard quarter of *Naiad*.
	Sailing caique (already reported) bearing 149.
1125	10 Ju 87 starboard quarter of *Naiad* in two waves of five.
1126	1 Ju 87 overhead power diving on *Naiad*.
1127	1 near miss port beam. 1 bomb off port beam.
	Near miss starboard side.
	Near miss starboard side.
	Near miss starboard quarter.
1129	4 near misses.
1130	6 near misses starboard side.
	5 near misses port side (water thrown onboard).
1131	Near miss starboard quarter. Aircraft machine-gunning decks of *Naiad*.
1136	5 near misses starboard quarter of *Naiad*.
	3 near misses port side of *Naiad*.
1137	4 well over port side of *Naiad*.
1139	Force C coming to support.
	Making water in topman's mess deck.
.	
1140	1 bomb 50 yards starboard side of *Naiad*.
1141	1 stick close starboard quarter of *Naiad*.
	Remainder of Force C opening fire and closing rapidly.
1143	1 bomb astern.
1145	Eased down to 20 knots owing to flooding.
	Remainder of Force C now in company.
1147	*Naiad's* RDF aerials gone. Jettisoning depth charges.
1150	16 knots slowing up.
1200	A magazine pierced and flooded.
1201	Ju 88 on port side. Destroyers opened fire.
1206	*Carlisle* opened fire.
1207	2 aircraft either troop carriers or torpedo bombers on starboard quarter of *Naiad*.
1208	1 dive bomber on port quarter of *Naiad*.
	2 dive bombers attacking *Carlisle*.
1209	Opened fire 2 large bombs astern of *Perth*.
1210	Ju 87 diving on *Naiad* but turned away.
1220	1 unknown steamer bearing 138.
1222	*Carlisle* opening fire.
1229	*Naiad* opened fire on Ju 88.
	1 large bomb off port quarter of *Carlisle*.

1229	2 bombs near *Carlisle* (? *Calcutta*)).
1235	5 bombs on *Carlisle* 1 hit amidships.
1243	Pom-poms opened fire.
1244	2 aircraft coming up astern of *Naiad*.
1245	4 bombs dropped a long way off to port of *Naiad*.
	Carlisle still under control and firing.
1246	1 aircraft coming up astern of *Naiad*.
1250	3 bombs close astern of *Calcutta*.
	3 torpedo bombers dead ahead of *Naiad*.
1252	2 bombs astern of *Calcutta* (Ju 88).
	Bad miss on *Calcutta* (Ju 88).
1258	Torpedo bomber dropped torpedo on port beam of *Naiad*.
1259	Torpedo passed under stern of *Naiad*.
1301	3 bombs astern of *Nubian*.
1303	1 bomb off starboard bow of *Naiad*.
1304	2 bombs astern of *Calcutta*.
1306	2 torpedo bombers waiting to attack.
1307	2 bombs off port side of *Calcutta*.
1315	1 torpedo dropped.
1316	1 stick astern of *Perth*.
1321	Battle fleet sighted bearing 240 18 miles.
1335	Altered course to 230.
1336	Bombing attack on battlefleet. *Warspite* hit.
1347	*Greyhound* sinking sailing Caique.
1348	2 groups of Ju 87's coming in from port quarter, 5 aircraft in each group.
1351	Opened fire.
	12 bombs dropped on *Greyhound*. 1 direct hit.
1353	*Greyhound* blew up; about 21 bombs round her.
1354	Stick of bombs round *Carlisle*.
1400	*Greyhound* turning over.
1445	Altered course to 190.
1500	18 knots.
1510	Opened fire.
1629	Aircraft in sight on beam of *Calcutta*, *Naiad* opened fire.
	7 aircraft port side. Fleet opened fire.
1633	5 bombs dropped astern of *Nubian*.
1634	8 bombs dropped ½ mile beyond *Carlisle*. All high level.
1636	*Nubian* opened fire on aircraft on port bow.
1639	*Warspite* opened fire.
	Stick of bombs round starboard destroyer of screen.
1641	*Naiad* opened fire.
1642	Stick of bombs on horizon.
1644	4 bombs close round *Valiant*.
1726	Altered course to 190.
1735	Aircraft bearing 110 closing.
1745	Altered course 215, 14 knots.
	Valiant opened fire on single aircraft.
1755	Single dive bomber diving on *Warspite*. Battle fleet opened fire, bombs dropped between *Warspite* and *Valiant*.
1812	*Valiant* opened fire on single dive bomber.
1815	*Naiad* opened fire. 3 bombs dropped well away from *Valiant*.
1930	Altered course 170.
1940	ZZ No 10.
2021	Taking up station astern of *Warspite*.

CHAPTER 9

The sinking of *Naiad*

Here dead lie we because we did not choose
To live and shame the land from which we sprang.
Life, to be sure, is nothing much to lose:
But young men think it is, and we were young.

A E Housman

BETWEEN THE COMPLETION OF *Naiad's* repairs in 1941 after Crete and her being torpedoed nine months later she was continuously in action against aircraft, submarines, surface ships and, in the Syrian war, shore batteries. During the Greek and Cretan campaigns German forces had penetrated Syria. Further, General Dentz, the commanding Vichy general, was known to be violently anti-British. Axis control of Syria would isolate Turkey and threaten both the Haifa oil terminal and perhaps even Egypt, another crisis for General Wavell to overcome.

Initially intelligence was scarce and it was even hoped - mistakenly - that French troops would come over to the Allies. By the time *Naiad* reached Haifa the army was held up on land and the RAF, Fleet Air Arm and Royal Navy heavily outnumbered. Just up the coast in Beirut were several powerful French destroyers which, with French aircraft, had already nearly sunk three of the few serviceable British destroyers while *Phoebe* narrowly missed being torpedoed by a French submarine. Before and after reaching the Syrian coast there were a number of significant German bomber raids on the ships as well as Haifa. The squadron's task was to bombard the French positions, then under attack by British and Australian soldiers. Often we were harried by French and German aircraft until the invasion of Russia, when the latter disappeared from our waters. Soon afterwards the RAF was reinforced and proved more than a match for the French.

Because of shortage of ships, Admiral King had been instructed to help the army rather than destroy the French naval force. Dermot Gard, *Naiad's* and the squadron's torpedo officer, put it to the admiral that, with the engineers' help, other means might be contrived to reduce the bothersome French destroyers bombarding British land forces nightly. Gard's idea was to attach a torpedo by some form of release gear, which I was to produce, to one of the Arab fishing boats in Haifa harbour. Then he and I and a couple of volunteers, disguised as fishermen, would work our way north and fish off Beirut where the French squadron lay. Hopefully, one of the three powerful French destroyers would come into our sights and, if my release and Gard's torpedo worked, be sunk. Luckily the admiral decided he could not wait so, after a Fleet Air Arm Swordfish operating from Cyprus successfully sank one of the French destroyers, he decided to take on the other two as they came south in the dark to attack Allied positions.

Marshall, my chief, was on leave so, for the first time, I bore 'all the machinery weight' during this not very famous action against the *Valmy* and the *Guépard*. Our quite powerful force of *Naiad*, *Phoebe* and several destroyers encountered the French as planned, exchanging a quite remarkable number of shells and torpedoes. Undoubtedly we scored some hits and they did not, but neither French destroyer was sunk. Concluding, on their return to Beirut, that discretion was valour's better part, they made tracks for France. In the end, presumably, these two fine vessels with a speed of 40 knots plus were scuttled. The French submarine, *Souffleur*, which had so nearly torpedoed *Phoebe*, was sunk about the same time by the British submarine *Parthian*.

Ashore the Allied, particularly Australian, troops were fighting their way towards Beirut. In early July they prepared to capture Damour which entailed our forces crossing a deep, rocky wadi (ravine) at the end of which there was a powerful French battery, our target and that of *HMAS Perth*, the staunch Australian six-inch-gunned cruiser with whom we had shared the battle beyond Crete. After hard fighting by the army the French defences crumbled and the way to Beirut lay open. By July 10 there was an armistice.

A week later we anchored off Acre as a communication link

for General Maitland Wilson, who had conducted this small but difficult campaign. A day or two afterwards a convention was signed ashore permitting the French an honourable capitulation. However General Dentz and those of his troops who wished to be repatriated to France were banned from leaving until British prisoners captured in the campaign and sent by Dentz to German prison camps were handed back.

After our Cretan experiences Haifa was a tonic, with sightseeing expeditions into Palestine for whoever could be spared. As we were moored alongside in harbour fuelling was made easy and our coastal trips used up few boiler hours. There was good drinking water ashore so our evaporators could be given much needed maintenance. If restaurants were expensive, the weather was balmy and bathing excellent. Haifa had a sense of history: the castles built by our crusading ancestors could still be visited. I seem to recall, too, that a consignment of fine chianti, bound for the Duke of Aosta in Eritrea, had been captured and was lying in bond. How our wardroom wine caterer or Amos our hostilities-only wine steward, once the Marquess of Salisbury's footman, acquired a supply I never knew, but we toasted the duke economically and enthusiastically. Haifa also gave me time to think about our battle organisation which had stood its test despite casualties among our experienced senior ratings, one killed and three badly wounded. Some older men looked worn and were probably over indulging by (illegally) purchasing tots of rum from those less inclined to drink their own. The real stalwarts seemed unshakeable, old Lambkin of the steering gear was one such. The main problem was loneliness. To be a watchkeeper, alone in a machinery compartment, in a ship undergoing intensive bombing or torpedo attack was itself an ordeal. How to double up at times of maximum stress, when our manpower reserves were small and some of our best stokers in hospital in Alexandria was a daunting problem made more difficult as their reliefs, strange to the ship, had yet to adjust to our ways.

All this, coupled with the gradually diminishing expertise below as a result of casualties, meant more close supervision from chief petty officers and officers alike. Our warrant engineers were rocks, but one was showing his age. The RN officer who had entered from university had found his feet and competently ran our damage control. The two RNVRs, although conscientious, needed supervision and still found it difficult to relax with the stokers. Commander Marshall and I had cabins above the after engine room but we decided that, at sea, we must separate. So at night I set up a camp bed by the forward (controlling) engine room hatch where I could hear any engine room telegraph orders and be instantly available to the officer of the watch if trouble occurred. We broke what were then the rules and trained stokers to take over the throttles, thus freeing skilled artificers and mechanicians to watch machinery for early symptome of failure. So far only one of our ship's company, sadly an officer, had broken down and had been removed, but in our department Marshall and I hoped careful management and sympathetic leadership would prevent a similar occurrence. Storey, the gunnery officer, was similarly engaged with the magazine crews who also worked below the waterline, well aware that in the case of fire their magazine would be flooded with them in it. But in action as we generally were, they had so much to do physically that there was little time to let imaginations run riot.

From Haifa we returned to Alexandria for a few days. By June 1941 vast convoys of men and materiel were reaching Suez via the Cape and a few German bombers were having a field day. They had already destroyed the *SS Georgic* after the troops' disembarkation and she was now beached. The *Queen Mary* and *Queen Elizabeth*, each with 15,000 troops on board, and halfway up the Red Sea, needed our protection on the last leg of their voyage. So *Naiad* was detailed to transit the Suez canal and reinforce the AA defences before the *Queens* entered the Gulf of Suez and while they were unloading.

There was a snag. Besides bombing Suez the Germans were determined to mine the canal. To cope with this threat nets had been strung across it, not to catch the mines but to indicate by the holes, just where mines had dropped. The night before *Naiad* was due to transit the canal such a hole was discovered but despite every effort the mine could not be located before we arrived. *Naiad* was ordered to stop all machinery (a patent impossibility) and muster the ship's company on the upper deck, knees bent, as the ship 'freewheeled' over the danger spot. We sent as many on deck as could be spared while, for the sake of those still below, the chief remained in the controlling engine room and I loitered in a boiler room where there were some very young new stokers on watch. Neither Marshall nor I, nor our companions in our hot temporarily fanless nether world, felt it necessary to adopt the half crouch position of those up top. If the mine exploded we would hit the deckhead hard enough whatever our stance, but for as much as we could of the five minutes it took to transit the danger area we held our breath. Sadly no one thought to photograph those from the admiral and captain down holding their rather lavatorial stance on the upper deck. It was, we were told, a majestic sight. On our return a week later a small tanker ahead of us detonated the mine but bravely got herself into the bank before sinking, thus allowing *Naiad* to pass safely with her crew in a more orthodox position.

Naiad had to go flat out to keep up with the *Queens* in the hot water of the Red Sea and Gulf of Suez. Towards the end of the voyage, instead of gradually easing down speed as was normal the telegraphs went from Full Speed to Stop: apparently an emergency. Correctly, a new and keen young artificer, anxious to show his alertness, opened up gland steam to the main turbines to maintain vacuum but failed first to drain the steam collector, and so injected cold water onto a very hot turbine rotor which shrank a few thousandths of an inch. When ordered astern the turbine jammed and *Naiad* headed blithely for the Suez beaches. Happily this disaster occurred only in one engine room, so with the other two shafts now at Full Astern we just missed hitting Egypt and journeyed back to Alexandria on two propellers. Two artificer/stoker teams later worked 12 hours on, 12 hours off for five days dismantling main steam pipes, lifting the turbine covers, readjusting the turbines, now slightly worn at their blade tips, and boxing them up before replacing and rejointing the pipes. I was lucky not to be court-martialled.

The decimation of our Mediterranean fleet resulted in the temporary abandonment of attempts to resupply Malta from Alexandria. The tanks we had brought out in Operation Tiger were now used by the army in Operation Battleaxe whose main aim was to force back Rommel, relieve Tobruk and recapture some airfields thus enabling fighter cover to be provided for Malta convoys. *Naiad* saw nothing of this but Rommel forced the army back to its start line and many of Winston's Tiger Cubs, which we had brought out, were lost. For the ensuing months Malta had to be supplied from the west and the aircraft carrier *Ark Royal*, as well as a cruiser were sunk, and *Nelson* and two other cruisers and two destroyers also damaged, hit by torpedo.

Our eastern Mediterranean operations now centred on Tobruk

and its build-up for a winter offensive by land. From Malta, Force K of cruisers and destroyers, *Upholder* commanded by Malcolm Wanklyn VC, DSO and two bars and other equally brave submarine crews constantly attacked and sank Rommel's supplies. *Naiad, Phoebe, Carlisle, Coventry* and *Galatea* drew too much water to enter Tobruk but for weeks we provided anti-aircraft cover for the smaller ships which could. So dangerous was their passage and so heavy their losses, that the Tobruk loading jetty in Alexandria was commonly known as the condemned cell. In August, for good political reasons, the navy had first to replace 6000 Australian troops and, in the ensuing two months, another 14,000 soldiers including the Polish Brigade were inserted and a similar number brought back to Alexandria, in addition to delivering 4000 tons of stores and ammunition. The strain on the cruisers was as nothing compared to the constant small ship casualties and losses. Expenditure of ammunition was colossal and our gun barrels had frequently to be renewed.

Naiad's casualties slowly mounted which meant visits, when we could spare the time, to the 64th General Hospital. On board, our various precautions against mental and physical wear and tear among our stokers and artificers seemed to be paying off. Nevertheless, in the middle of one fairly intense bombing attack I found one of our most stalwart engine room watchkeepers curled up and weeping bitterly. Each of us has only a finite store of fortitude. The trick, I convinced myself, was to change people's jobs. But it was not easy either to assess whose credit was getting low, or how to provide an adequate substitute. Still more supervision found its way upwards onto shoulders already overburdened. At least our skill at patching splinter holes, appearing anywhere not covered by our good Czechoslovakian steel armoured belt, improved and began to make us look as though we had measles.

There was little night life ashore and anyway we were always at short notice from midnight. But Pastroudis restaurant saw us sometimes and my cousins' ever open houses allowed me to meet some of the splendid Long Range Desert Group back from some foray. In the summer, our admiral, still a total stranger, left the 15th cruiser squadron in the hands of our captain until Rear-Admiral Vian of *Cossack* fame joined us in October.

Vian did not commend himself to us at first. We were a happy wardroom with complete trust in our navigator, John Forbes, and his capacity so to control *Naiad* that the bombs missed. Forbes was also Staff Officer Operations but unfortunately Vian had brought his own SOO, Lieutenant Commander Maurice, an agreeable but rather bald officer, and Forbes had to leave. Unlike his predecessor Vian lost no time in visiting the wardroom. When introduced to Storey, our irrepressible gunnery officer, Vian remarked grimly (but not altogether accurately), *It's about time you got your hair cut, Gunnery Officer.*

Most would have shrivelled at this peremptory rebuke, but Australians are made of sterner stuff. Not at all put out Storey replied, *Certainly not, sir. Having now met your SOO I think we need all we can grow.*

The admiral scowled but it was a measure of his understanding of men that, until the end of the Pacific War nearly four years later, he kept Storey with him as a confidante and staff officer.

Soon after taking command Vian agreed to bombard Benghazi harbour and some of Rommel's supply ships, to coincide with our army's mid-November advance. As we heard afterwards few on the bridge thought *Naiad* would survive. Although considerable damage was done to harbour installations enemy bombing was as fierce as anything we had known and many were wounded, though none killed. Mutiny is an ugly word and there was no question of that for thanks to Kelsey, Dowling and Marshall and others at the top, *Naiad* was still a very happy ship. However, the messdecks took against the admiral and his SOO to whom some of the blame was quite unjustly attributed. It was known too that Vian had quarrelled with our captain over camouflage. If Captain Kelsey was not particularly inspiring he was known to be both kindly and lucky. It so happened that he was a camouflage fan and Warrant Shipwright Irish was often maddened by Kelsey's demands for paintings of *Naiad* against different sky backgrounds. The captain's constant attempts to make us invisible or, at least, less vulnerable to air attack were well known and appreciated by all.

A spotless quarterdeck in the sunny Mediterranean made a splendid target. While Kelsey commanded our squadron *Naiad's* quarterdeck was given a dark green wash and the ship's sides and funnels so grotesquely coloured that a splendidly caustic signal from Cunningham himself was received. When Vian came on board, quite forgetting that he was no longer a destroyer captain, he ordered the quarterdeck to be holystoned. Kelsey intimated that it was his ship and the quarterdeck would remain painted. The row then disappeared into the admiral's cabin and my chief was sent for. I was later instructed to contrive saltwater sprays to be used at sea, whereby the quarterdeck would be kept wet and therefore fairly dark. But in harbour the deck was to be in its peacetime pristine condition. All this added to the murmurings as much extra work was involved. How Vian became aware of what was being said I don't know, but he had brought with him his able seaman cabin hand who was probably the source. Once Vian heard what was being said about the Benghazi action he acted promptly and addressed the ship's company. He told them that the intensity of the bombing *Naiad* had weathered off Benghazi was heavier than he had ever met before and that he now understood Mediterranean conditions much better. Although he could never guarantee that such attacks would not be repeated he realised *Naiads* were much more used to them than he was, he would certainly not invite such a battle again. Vian's honesty and admissions restored his standing with the lower deck and he became admired not only for the reputation he brought with him but for his obvious leadership. In many ways Vian did us much good. We were tending to become bomb happy and discipline was slipping. His resolute and uncompromising attitude to dress and behaviour was a tonic to us all.

By accident I was reputed to have given the admiral his desserts after the Benghazi bombing. He had sent orders that he would always require a hot meal as soon as the ship stood down from action stations. But the admiral's galley was oil-fired and because, long before Vian joined, we had had a serious fire when a molten splinter hit the oil gravity tank it was always emptied at sea. Experimentation by the leading stoker responsible showed that if he ran a pump in a boiler room for two minutes there would be enough oil to cook with and little danger of fire should an attack develop. Unfortunately, during the Benghazi action, the stoker concerned was badly wounded and his stand-in less skilled. As we entered Alexandria harbour the flag lieutenant was triumphantly informed that the meal was ready. Vian left the bridge. At the bottom of the bridge ladder Vian's feet flew from under him and he was deposited in a pool of diesel oil from the tank overflow. Like Cunningham Vian always wore correct uniform which happened to be white so the result was catastrophic. My subsequent meeting with Philip Vian was not a happy one.

November 1941 started reasonably well for us and the Cyprus garrison of 15, 000 men was changed over. On November 18 the Allied army attacked in the western desert but made slow progress. Three days later the Tobruk garrison broke out prematurely and Rommel prevented their linking up with our forces from Egypt. At sea the 15th cruiser squadron was engaged in protecting our store ships bound for Mersa Matruh and bombarding the coast between Derna and Bardia. On November 25 the squadron was near the British battlefleet searching for an Italian convoy when *Barham* was torpedoed, blew up and sank. Two days later *HMAS Parramatta,* carrying Dick Litchfield, my Dartmouth prop, was also torpedoed escorting an ammunition ship to the beleaguered Tobruk garrison. Happily the ammunition ship won through but only 20 of *Parramatta's* crew survived and Dick Litchfield was not amongst them. Other store ships were attacked and many sunk. As we now know some 20 German submarines had entered the Mediterranean in October.

In December *Naiad* was almost continuously in action either bombarding the coast or trying to intercept Rommel's convoys and returned to harbour only to re-fuel, re-ammunition and land our wounded. The army's advance slowed and Tobruk was not finally relieved until December 8, two days after we had heard that Japanese aircraft had destroyed most of the American Pacific fleet in Pearl Harbour. On December 10 we learned of the destruction of the *Prince of Wales* and *Repulse* off Malaya. On December 14 as we were entering the swept channel into Alexandria, the *Galatea*, immediately ahead of us, was hit by two torpedoes and sank almost instantly. Somehow we avoided the wreckage and the swimmers but the smoke and smell of the explosion was sucked down by the fans into our machinery spaces. She took with her Commander (E) Lancelot Fogg-Elliott who had been the chief of *Forres*, our coal-fired Dartmouth training sloop, the man who, as senior of the *Hood*, had shown me how an engine room department should be run.

Next night we were off with a small force to fight through the gallant *Breconshire* and her cargo of oil for Malta. Her captain, Hutchison, was a particular friend of ours. On December 17 as we neared Malta in the middle of a furious attack by bombers and torpedo bombers, we sighted Italian battleships and cruisers between us and our destination. Sending *Breconshire* away to the south with a small escort under a smokescreen, Vian led us into attack. I was in the superstructure inspecting some massive splinter damage to our boiler room fan intakes, when the news of the Italian battleships was broadcast. With the help of the damage control sentry, I quite improperly opened the screen door to see what was happening. At that moment a 15in salvo straddled us and a splinter removed an eighth of an inch from Stoker Janes' chin. Having hastily secured the door and escorted him to the nearest first aid post I went below where, inexplicably, life seemed safer. By the time I reached the engine room we had increased to full speed, were opening fire at extreme range and, as we could see from the rudder indicator, were weaving to dodge the incoming salvos and bombs. Vian had taken the precaution the day before of dispatching *Carlisle* and two destroyers to break wireless silence and simulate the approach of a British battlefleet. Whether it was this or our determined attack, the Italian force, which far outnumbered us, turned away in the gathering dusk and made off. So ended the first battle of Sirte. Ordered back to Alexandria we just avoided a major attack by Wellington bombers, sent out to destroy the Italian force which they mistook for us. But Hutchison and his *Breconshire* reached Malta with her precious cargo of fuel oil.

In the ensuing hours, Force K under Captain Rory O'Conor (my old commander in *Hood*) in *Neptune* searching for an Italian convoy, ran into a minefield. First *Neptune* was damaged and, after drifting for many hours, hit three more mines and sank with the loss of all but one of her crew. Then, *Kandahar* hit a mine and sank but a most gallant effort by *Jaguar* saved a fair number of her company. The fleet's Calvary was not over. On returning from our encounter with the Italian fleet and the Wellington bombers and because of *Galatea's* loss a few days before, our destroyer escort were spread around the swept channel to Alexandria in an anti-submarine sweep. The cruisers and destroyers entered and the boom was closed. Whether this procedure meant that the boom was open for longer than usual I don't know, but we had hardly got steam off main engines when we were warned enemy frogmen might be in the harbour. All ships were to lower boats and drop small charges in the water as a deterrent.

There would be no further sleep that night.

As dawn broke our weary sailors rowed round the ship (the motor boat had been riddled with splinters) while our gunner dropped charges rather too close for the nerves of my dynamo watchkeepers. The first whoomph came just before 0600 and an oiler, only two berths away, with *Jervis* alongside, was clearly down by the stern. From the speed with which *Jervis* got clear there was hope that she was undamaged. Then came news that the battleship *Valiant* had discovered two enemy frogmen and had incarcerated them low down, for'd. Shortly they asked to come on deck and reported that they had placed a charge under *Valiant's* A turret timed to go off in a few minutes. We smartly retreated to *Naiad's* port side away from *Valiant*. Luckily the explosive had dropped off into the mud under *Valiant*, which was holed when the charge went off without detonating A magazine.

Soon after *Valiant* had settled onto the bottom there was a horrendous thud and a vast pall of smoke billowed up from *Queen Elizabeth's* funnel as the fleet flagship took a heavy list to starboard. Two submarines were brought alongside to provide electric power and counter-flooding brought her back to an even keel but now also on the mud with a 40ft-hole in one boiler room. The brave Italian frogmen were incarcerated for six months in the hope that the fleet's true state would be kept from our enemies, for now Cunningham had little left.

As 1942 opened the army reached beyond Benghazi which gave us the opportunity to run more fuel into Malta in the *Glengyle* and bring back the *Breconshire*. A further convoy of four ships set sail a few days later. One was sunk by bombs although we managed to push the others through including *Breconshire* and bring back the *Glengyle* and the *Rowallan Castle*. At this moment Rommel attacked El Agheila. Benghazi, just restored to working order and restocked by the navy with petrol, had to be abandoned on January 25 and the fuel destroyed. Derna fell quickly and with it the possibility of air cover for our Malta convoys.

In mid-February Cunningham determined to try to run a really big convoy into Malta. *Naiad* set off with *Euryalus, Dido, Carlisle* and seven Hunt and eight Fleet destroyers, with *Clan Campbell, Clan Chattan* and *Rowallan Castle*. *Penelope*, the last remaining cruiser of Force K at Malta, managed to deliver *Breconshire* and three empty merchant ships to us in return, but despite the expenditure of nearly 4000 rounds of 5.25 ammunition and the destruction of several enemy bombers, both *Clan Chattan* and *Rowallan Castle* were disabled and had to be sunk. The *Clan Campbell*, badly damaged, just managed to reach Tobruk. So the attempt failed and we returned with many casualties, our magazines

• *Naiad in Alexandria shortly before setting off for Malta on her last convoy*

near empty and the ships' companies exhausted. The battle for Crete had cost the navy more than 2000 men 'Discharged Dead'. In the following seven months up to Christmas the fleet lost 500 killed or missing and 250 wounded, to which had to be added *Barham's* 900 dead and another 2000 or more lost in *Galatea, Neptune, Kandahar, Jackal,* the U-class submarines from Malta and some of the T-class from Alexandria. A total of about 6000 besides many wounded.

Naiad's many wounded were accomodated in the 64th General Hospital. I found it encouraged me to visit them in those dark days, despite a tiresomely long hot journey by tram, as they were ever cheerful. Many wanted me to intercede with the doctors to return them to the ship quickly. My family call my occasional fits of depression Gaskell Gloom, after my authoress ancestor Mrs Gaskell, a gloomy lady, but as I left the hospital on March 9 an able young artificer, who had teased me on a previous trip for not wearing my lifebelt (just a rubber tyre in those days worn around one's chest uninflated and a frightful encouragement to prickly heat) called out, *Don't forget to wear your lifebelt this time, sir. We look forward to your visits.* A shiver similar to that I had experienced on the Nigg golf course nine years before ran down my spine. All the way back in the rickety tram I could not shake off the feeling of imminent crisis. After a strong whisky at my cousins' ever open house, I made my way to Ras el Tin for the 1930 boat back to *Naiad.* Within a few yards of the ship an Egyptian tug, rounding *Naiad's* stern too fast, rammed our boat amidships and continued into the night. Happily the buoyancy tanks kept us afloat and, though we all got a ducking in Alexandria's filthy harbour and a considerable fright, we struggled to the gangway.

A further and even stronger whisky dispersed my gloom altogether. The crisis, I felt, was past. Captain Kelsey had departed on promotion to be replaced by Captain Guy Grantham, the first public school term officer at Dartmouth, a submariner by trade. Until she had been hit by a torpedo and had departed to the States for repairs, he had captained our sister ship *Phoebe*. Recovering from our ducking, we absorbed with alcoholic equanimity the news that we were all to sail at 0400 to seek a damaged Italian cruiser. If we failed to find her then we were to escort another sister ship *Cleopatra* (like *Naiad* a Hawthorn Leslie product) which was out of ammunition in Malta.

Vian had instituted a leave roster and was adamant that a small number of us should spend a few days away in a Palestinian rest camp. Splendid in theory and certainly much needed this complicated our problems below. Because we had just lost the irreplaceable Tom Browell, our superlative warrant engineer to a destroyer, relieved by a splendid qualified young Keyham officer, we sent only some of the older artificers and petty officers, although their absence would be felt.

At first all went well and, though the squadron saw no sign of the Italian cruiser, the virtually unarmed *Cleopatra* was successfully transferred to her three class-mates. Sailors are always deeply superstitious and the 15th cruiser squadron believed that whenever four of the *Dido* class were in company one would sink or be badly damaged. First there had been *Dido, Euryalus, Phoebe* and *Bonaventure* until the latter was sunk. Then there were *Naiad, Euryalus, Phoebe* and *Dido* until *Dido* was bombed and had to be sent to America for repairs. When *Naiad, Euryalus, Dido* and *Phoebe* sailed again *Phoebe* had to retire to the States, badly hurt by torpedo. That we now had *Naiad, Euryalus, Dido* and *Cleopatra* was bad enough for the messdeck gloomies but when our new captain, who had been liaison officer with the army since *Phoebe* left and must have forgotten what was so implicitly believed, cheerfully broadcast early on March 11 that, *Once more the 15th Cruiser Squadron is all the same class*, a frisson ran through the ship. Within minutes the most intensive bombing attack we had endured since Benghazi began, and continued for nine and a half hours.

An hour after dark when the bombing was over we went back to cruising stations and some were relaxing in the wardroom when depth charges were heard. Vian's orders by night were that

• *A near miss on Naiad's stern*

if any of the destroyer screen suspected a submarine that ship was to burn a searchlight for a few seconds. This would alert the admiral to turn the force towards the threat and perhaps comb the track of any torpedoes. Unluckily the destroyer that suddenly sighted a submarine on the surface had come straight from the UK and raised the alarm by auxiliary wave radio. By the time her position on the screen was established, it was too late for any avoiding action. One torpedo missed just ahead, another astern and the third hit *Naiad* amidships.

As the torpedo exploded and all lights went out my chief and I were by the after engine room hatch where I saw him putting on all the clips on the for'd bulkhead door, thus effectively sealing off the damage. In the design of the *Dido* class, as previously mentioned too prone to sink quickly, no machinery compartment had direct access to the upper deck. Anyone trapped and lacking vertical access had the choice of opening a watertight door to a passage or drowning. Against orders we had already cut manholes through the gratings at the top of each boiler room through which, in fact, all in the flooded boiler room got away, but there were other machinery spaces and compartments from which there was no escape. My feeling of guilt that I had not broken the rules earlier and rectified this deplorable design fault probably accounts in part for the guerrilla warfare I have sometimes waged against the Royal Corps of Naval Constructors. In a few cases, to achieve vertical access, it would have meant major dockyard work. But if we had done for the dynamo rooms and a few other spaces what we did for the boiler rooms more lives might have been saved.

Desperately burned though some of them were, we managed to extract a few before the for'd engine room flooded. That we extricated so many was due to a newly-joined RNVR officer who, at the cost of savage burns to his face and hands, shut off the emergency steam valve thus saving many from being flayed alive by superheated steam. John Smith somehow survived to become a top scientist in the Atomic Energy Authority.

We now had steam in the for'd boiler room and main engines in the after engine room between which lay a fractured steam line. Two dynamos were destroyed and the other two could get no steam while an emergency diesel, which should have been part of the original design, had arrived only the day before we sailed and was not yet wired up. In one way or another *Naiad* was doomed and would have probably have had to be sunk by our own forces. But though, to begin with, we had a considerable list to starboard, we should have continued to float. Later, as I made my way to the bridge to tell the captain the state of affairs, the ship lurched to starboard almost onto her beam ends and the order of *Abandon Ship* given. Despite the navy's many losses no directive had been made recommending which side, the high or the low, should be used when taking to the water. Except for those on the bridge or

• *Naiad survivors aboard HMS Jervis the morning after*

superstructure the lower side appeared the more frightening lest the ship should roll on top of you. Yet the high side, we soon discovered, carried its own perils: barnacles and the bilge keels had to be surmounted. As the ship sank lower in the water that night I found myself on her side with our newly-joined USN liaison officer. We had a polite parley.

After you , sir. No, after you , sir, guests first.

Ahead of me he broke his ankle on the bilge keel while somehow I reached the water unscathed. The sea seemed rough but not too cold as we strove to distance ourselves from *Naiad's* loom to avoid suction. There were one or two Carley floats about into which we tried to put the wounded and those who had forgotten their lifebelts. There seemed little hope of rescue. The force had been doing 20 knots or more and the admiral commanding was in the water. Obviously it would take time for someone to assume control and, with submarines about, the destroyers would be more than ever needed if the rest of the squadron was to survive. Against the starry sky we saw *Naiad's* bows rear up before she slipped slowly back into the depths. We gave her a small cheer: we had been through a lot together.

For an hour or so we swam around, trying to help those inclined to panic, although most were strangely calm. We spoke of our happy times and the rough ones. Many near me were stoker, artificer and mechanician friends from Tyneside days but others were more recently joined, less resigned to what seemed a hopeless situation and in need of jollying along. Hope and encouragement we tried to give them but the more battle-weary, I believe, quietly accepted that we would float till welcome sleep bore us away. When a destroyer hove in sight all changed. Life suddenly seemed precious again as we swam towards the jumping nets over the ship's side and the shouts of encouragement. We knew that at any moment her Asdic might detect a submarine, when she would drive off at full speed and release depth charges with results too awful for us to contemplate. Some made it while for others the final effort was too much or the sea too rough. The last I believe to reach *Jervis'* side I had no strength left to haul myself up. Her chief, Commander (E) later Rear Admiral Henry Hogger, seeing a white overall struggling at the bottom of the jumping net, climbed down and with a sailor's help hauled me on board. *Jervis*, then commanded by Captain Mack, had experienced this routine many times before and their drill was perfect.

We were stripped, the oil fuel washed from our eyes and bodies, and each given a blanket or clothing. After a blessed tot of rum Marshall, I and the paymaster son of the King's Private Secretary fell asleep on the floor and across the captain's ample bed, a present from Hawthorn Leslie, *Jervis'* builder as well as *Naiad's*.

It took two boards of enquiry to establish why *Naiad* sank. We were low of course both in oil and ammunition and therefore unstable but our watertight door discipline was good and we should have stayed afloat. The torpedo had hit the ship under a bathroom, where those just off watch were washing. Most were killed or suffered broken legs but one strong young man with a shattered ankle seized a junior artificer with two broken legs, carried him into the passage and, as there was no vertical access, managed to unclip the watertight door my chief had closed. He and his wounded friend escaped to the upper deck and both survived. But the watertight door left open allowed the flooding to pour along the main starboard passage aft until *Naiad* was on her beam ends.

Later Admiral Cunningham wrote to the first sea lord.

Such a loss that little Naiad. A highly efficient weapon with a ship's company with a grand spirit. The four cruisers were bombed from nine to six-thirty without damage, and then to stumble on a submarine was just too sickening. The American liaison officer who sustained a broken ankle told me the behaviour of the ship's company was wonderful when she sank.

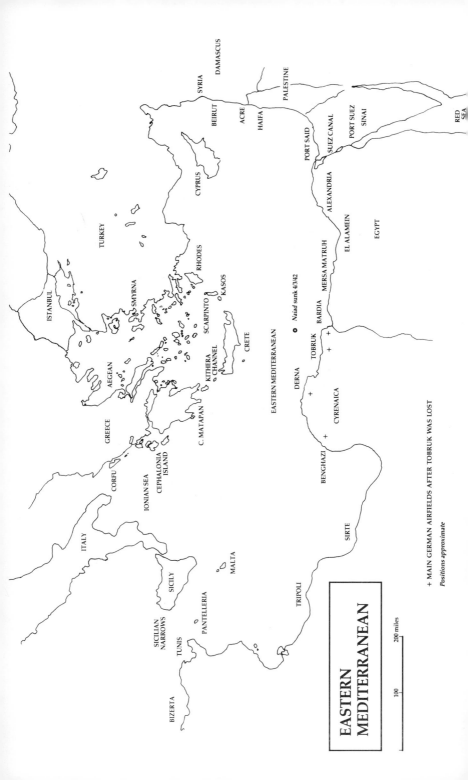

EASTERN
MEDITERRANEAN

+ MAIN GERMAN AIRFIELDS AFTER TOBRUK WAS LOST

Positions approximate

100   200 miles

RED SEA

DAMASCUS

SYRIA

PALESTINE

BEIRUT

ACRE

HAIFA

PORT SAID

SUEZ CANAL

PORT SUEZ

SINAI

CYPRUS

ALEXANDRIA

EGYPT

TURKEY

EL ALAMEIN

RHODES

MERSA MATRUH

SMYRNA

KASOS

BARDIA

SCARPINTO

○ *Naiad* sunk 4/3/42

TOBRUK +

EASTERN MEDITERRANEAN

CRETE

DERNA +

KITHERA CHANNEL

C. MATAPAN

CYRENAICA +

AEGEAN

GREECE

BENGHAZI

CORFU

IONIAN SEA

CEPHALONIA ISLAND

ISTANBUL

ITALY

SIRTE

MALTA

SICILY

PANTELLERIA

TRIPOLI

SICILIAN NARROWS

TUNIS

BIZERTA

CHAPTER 10

Keyham and Manadon, 1942-1944

Your endeavour should be to inspire in your men a feeling of respect for you and confidence in your sympathetic interest and understanding of their problems, as well as in your professional ability. This is the sure basis of discipline and leadership.

(Taken from the best practical guide to leadership that I have met. Written and circulated in 1937 to *HMS Hood's* officers by Captain, later Vice Admiral Sir Francis Pridham, KBE, CB)

DURING THE FIRST WAR two types of engineer officer were at sea; old type engineers whose entry had been stopped in 1910 and who carried the main burden of keeping the fleets serviceable and Fisher's new (E) specialists, gaining their bridge and engine room watchkeeping certificates on the job at sea but who received no other professional training until the war ended. Thus there was nearly a 10-year gap within the training cycle of engineers which contributed to the lack of a technologically up-to-date fleet at the start of world war two.

In 1939 the engineer-in-chief was determined that history should not repeat itself and ordered no change in Keyham's four year (11 terms) training of (E) specialist officers or in the shorter advanced course at RNC, Greenwich. Because of the flood of volunteers for naval officer entry immediately before and after the war's start, most entrants were of the highest calibre both intellectually and in leadership qualities and many opted for or were guided to Keyham. By the autumn of 1942, with the war entering its fourth year, a feeling akin to mutiny developed amongst these fine young men whose high intelligence had brought them into the (E) specialisation: they had not joined the navy to spend their time tackling physics and thermo-dynamics while their kin were fighting Germans. Many staff officers teaching them felt similarly.

Casualties amongst (E) officers early on had been considerable. Captain, later Rear-Admiral, (E) C H Nicholson whose sympathetic and often brilliant appointing expertise has rarely been recognised, had two options: the first was to send the experienced but often weary survivors back to sea in the hope that the casualty rate would diminish. The second was to accept the loss of valuable design and repair expertise by moving the incumbent (E) officers from the department of the engineer-in-chief, dockyards and training establishments, particularly Keyham, and substitute survivors who could be rested ashore before being sent back to sea again. Wherever he could he chose the latter course. Amongst such survivors were many bitter weeds who knew that the navy had gone to war unprepared strategically, tactically (night fighting apart) and above all technologically.

Thus towards the end of 1942 I found myself at Keyham with Lieutenants AE(P) Thackara, Illingworth and Mott, three of the first air engineering specialists to fight as front-line pilots. There were also Lewin from *Ilex*, last met nursing a badly damaged destroyer in Haifa, Ellum from *Aurora* and the rough world of Force K at Malta, Oliver from *Ark Royal*, sunk off Gibraltar due to a major design fault despite his remarkable personal efforts to save her, Wildish, later a great vice-admiral in the personnel field, from *Prince of Wales*, sunk by the Japanese off Malaya, whose father, later Engineer Rear-Admiral Sir Henry Wildish KBE, CB must also be numbered among the greats, for the whole burden of the serviceability of the Battle of the Atlantic escort forces rested on his shoulders, and Osborne from *Hotspur*, certainly the most battle-hardened of us all. We were led by Captain (E) B L G Sebastian, a Fisher-scheme officer and Commander (E) G R Cook, soon to become chief of *King George V*.

On the staff were several civilians who had tried to teach us only five years earlier, together with some well-known uniformed instructor officers, most famous of whom was Instructor Captain Darcy Lever. His marked eccentricity had led to his early retirement from the navy, but the recall of this ex-Trinity College, Cambridge wrangler to teach officers at Keyham benefitted all. His mathematics and physics lectures inspired the dullest even if his rather odd idea of uniform, a cap always worn in the mess with its badge askew, a barely sewn-on fourth stripe on one arm, set the young no dress example. Cambridge dons could surely thus behave; indeed it seemed to give the College a cachet to have such a revered and notable teacher around. His lectures out of hours on science and religion and the nature of space (to him a marvellous onomatopoeic word *blobbery*) helped our frustrated young men whose brothers were being killed in a war in which, seemingly, they were destined to play no part. His comments on the Doppler effect, as the bombs fell and he wandered around the firewatchers on the roof, were often very funny and always comforted the frightened. His consumption of gin was enormous, his capacity to interest prodigious, his performances on the double base or viola up to international concert standard, his kindness heartwarming.

Berthon's ideas five years earlier, that the College should move to Manadon, had been fulfilled but not in time to build other than a number of nissen huts and a small instructional block. The midshipmen messed in what is now the captain's residence, which also accomodated a number of staff officers. The wardroom was in what is now the guest bedroom. The midshipmen took rifles and ammunition to lectures against possible paratroop landings, a somewhat daunting experience for the lecturer as I quickly found. The rest of the officers were bussed two miles into Keyham each morning to join the duty watch of sub-lieutenant firewatchers and dispatch riders.

With nightly air raids and a mighty blitz on Plymouth, little sleep in unheated huts lacking water or conveniences, professional instruction somehow continued. The wonder was that Sebastian and Cook had kept things running at all. By 1942 Nicholson was organising a great clear out: those (E) officers who had reluctantly held shore appointments went to sea and their replacements, the bitter weeds from sea, started to inject their war experience.

Sebastian and Cook had unsuccessfully demanded that the Keyham course should be shortened. It was left to us to show that ships would welcome highly motivated midshipmen even with only a smattering of engineering knowledge. In addition, after experience of action at sea those who returned would be more amenable to the theoretical instruction they found so frustrating. Quickly it was decided that if the College could cram enough practical engineering into midshipmen in four terms then they could be sent to sea for a year or so before returning to complete their training. I was given the task of creating this syllabus. Others, more intellectually gifted, wrote a more advanced version for those on return from the fleet. I was told also to write a pamphlet entitled, *Hints for officers about to go to sea*, which developed such a wealth of apparently pompous clichés that I had to bring in a cartoonist friend to make it palatable. This activity, besides teaching disillusioned young officers who feared the war would end before they qualified, brought an added bonus. I was able to join various Home Fleet units, which now had the midshipmen for training, as an additional watchkeeper. At first hand I could see how the scheme was operating in practice and take aboard suggestions for its improvement. Despite the hair-raising flight from Donibristle to Hatston in the Orkneys, this let me escape the hothouse climate of a training establishment, as did my attachment to the Damage Control School which had taken over the premises of the Royal Ballet School near Baron's Court headed by the first of my Dartmouth term officers and Commander (E) Marshall from *Naiad*, as its second in command. To the DCS were sent many survivors whose tales of what-went-wrong were analysed and dispatched, via the Admiralty naval staff, to the design and training establishments. Fire was a great hazard at sea, but too much water could lead to 'free surface' flooding high up in a damaged ship thereby contributing to instability. For a short while I was seconded to the National Fire Service whose difficulties were somewhat analagous. Whereas we wished to put out fires with minimum water, the NFS often had to try to extinguish them with water supplies interrupted by bombing. Thus the variable spray nozzle, now used universally, came to be developed which led to the establishing of a primitive firefighting school at Manadon. There young (E) officers, closely involved with all aspects of damage control at sea, could practise the use of breathing apparatus and various methods of firefighting in restricted spaces.

With the allied armies racing towards Germany we Keyham instructors felt that it was time to rejoin the fleet. Repeated applications in response to the call for Special Service Volunteers were as repeatedly turned down by Admiral Nicholson, our appointer, with the words, *your turn will come*. To keep us quiet or because we were being fattened up for jobs normally beyond our seniority as lieutenants (E), several of us suddenly found ourselves 'Quasi-Acting Lieutenant-Commanders(E)' a title only a cautious Admiralty could have devised. This elevation which thankfully carried with it the appropriate pay rise was shortly followed by our appointments to Pacific-bound ships. I had drawn the job of senior engineer of *HMS Duke of York* refitting in Liverpool and due once again to become Admiral Fraser's flagship.

With escape in sight and believing that the Pacific campaign would be prolonged, I cancelled my trip to the Home Fleet in the summer of 1944 and took a leave warrant and rucksack to the farthest permitted spot in the British Isles. It was a glorious August and after two days in the train I found myself at Mallaig opposite Skye. Having provisioned I walked by Loch Morar and so to Glenfinnan, where I tarried for the next four days. There, for less than a pound a night for a huge breakfast, supper and sandwiches for my rucksack, I explored the higher reaches of the Finnan, watched stags and golden eagles and took refuge from the heat and the clegs in the ice-cold pools of the mountain streams. Then on to Fort William, Ballachulish and the Clachaig Inn next to the site of the Glencoe massacre. Buchaille Etive, Ossian's Cave, Bidean and other climbs got me fit again and, incidentally, left me relatively unharmed by a night at the King's House Inn on Rannoch Moor and a bottle of light-coloured liquid with a scrawled label 'Whisky'. And so back by bus and train for a few more weeks at Keyham.

It is difficult, after nearly 50 years, to assess whether we helped the Keyham and Manadon young to tolerate their appalling living conditions and give them a sense of purpose amid the dreary bookwork they endured. Some were disillusioned with the navy and left after the war: some now have their names inscribed on the Roll of Honour (one with the Albert Medal) at Manadon. Others, more fortunate, succeeded brilliantly. Midshipman (E) Stephens RCN finished his career as an admiral and Canadian member of the NATO Military Committee. Sub-Lieutenant (E) Reid RAN also became an admiral and third naval member of his country's Navy Board. Midshipman (AE) Bryson became the first (E) officer to join the Board of Admiralty as third sea lord and controller, president of the Institution of Electrical Engineers and lord lieutenant of East Sussex. Midshipman (E) Pillar served on the Board of Admiralty, became the first (E) officer to be commandant of the Royal College of Defence Studies, a member of the Royal Yacht Squadron and then lieutenant-governor of Jersey. Midshipman (E) Horlick excelled in the hot seat as a vice-admiral and director general (ships), during the

Falklands war.   Midshipman (later Rear-Admiral) Dymoke, before he engined the nuclear Polaris fleet, helped to point the way to an all-gas turbine navy.   Midshipman (E) Flower, as a commander, wrote the draft paper which persuaded the Board to accept gas turbine propulsion and ended his naval career as Port Admiral, Portsmouth.   Midshipman Hogg, as a commander, given the resources and unique over-riding authority to cut through red-tape, solved a crisis affecting the mobility of the more recently designed fleet at a particularly important moment, and ended his career as a rear-admiral.   Midshipman (AE) Titford became a rear-admiral and director of aircraft maintenance and repair; Midshipman (E) Lea a vice-admiral and master of the Plumber's Company.   Sub-Lieutenant (E) Pepper, invalided, became a director of Rolls-Royce and gave enormous help to Dymoke and the navy in the nuclear programme.   After the war Midshipman (E) Bailes then a Lieutenant (E) took six months' unpaid leave and sailed alone in a 25-ft Folkboat to New Zealand. Later, having left the navy and repeated his voyage, he has spent 30 years training the natives of the Pacific archipelagoes in navigation and marine engineering.   Sub-Lieutenants (E) Morgan and Parker moved up the ladder in BP; and Sub-Lieutenants (E) Bell and Good served brilliantly in the Yarrow Admiralty Research Department, while Good also was part of a small team which helped the Canadian government to build the *St Laurent* class in record time from a green field site to commissioned ships.   Midshipman John Pereira IN reached the rank of rear-admiral in the Indian navy and Midshipman Cruddas reached the rank of rear-admiral and, after steering the (British) Phantom programme to a successful conclusion in the States, became director-general aircraft.   The quality of the wartime intake was superlative and their patience remarkable.   All the teaching staff could do was to recognise their potential and try to inject some of the revolutionary fervour that Berthon, Sebastian and others had lit amongst a generation of (E) officers under training in the late twenties and early thirties, now fanned into flame by their war experiences.

CHAPTER 11

Japan surrenders

The war with Japan will end at 1200 on August 15. It is likely that kamikazes will attack the fleet after this time as a final fling. Any ex-enemy aircraft is to be shot down in a friendly manner.

C-in-C Third Fleet

MY APPOINTMENT AS Professor of Marine Engineering at Keyham ended in December 1944 – in hospital. This was the result of a poisoned scratch from the rugger field. After a painful interlude and two days' convalecence I travelled to Liverpool a week late to join *HMS Duke of York*. Those two days however were well spent as in the engineer-in-chief's department I met many of the officers I had come to call 'the revolutionaries'. United by their wartime experiences against the engineering hierarchy's opposition, they demanded a whole series of radical changes which ultimately transformed the navy's mobility.

The difficulties faced by our 'short legged' fleet, with *Duke of York* as flagship, in operating with the US navy in the Pacific were quickly made clear to me. Our ships, designed pre-war, were quite unsuited to the maritime strategy conducted by Admiral Nimitz USN in that vast ocean area. What could be done to help the British Pacific fleet had already been put in hand but the rest would be up to us. We had no fast tankers and even a reliable fleet train to support British ships was impossible. A dinner with Commander Cook, now chief of *King George V*, due to leave Liverpool three months ahead of *Duke of York*, brought me up to date. It was not only the future horrors of the Pacific we faced, there were current horrors in Cammell Laird's refit to be corrected.

It was not the firm's fault: many of their best men had been absorbed into the forces; the constant bombing of Liverpool had wearied everyone and the young were unskilled. The Winkles who had set the pace in Newcastle five years before had vanished.

My predecessor, Lieutenant Commander (E) Peter Walker, a brilliant engineer and later Vice Admiral Sir Peter Walker and chief naval engineer officer, as the engineer-in-chief came to be called, had won a well-earned DSC during the battle of the North Cape when the *Duke of York* sank the *Scharnhorst*. Despite his efforts the refit, not helped by my late arrival, had gone poorly.

A draft of petty officers and stokers, many of them Hostilities Only (HO) had arrived 24 hours before me instead of 10 days after by which time, had I not been delayed, I might have got some sort of grip. Some were determined to avoid their Pacific drafts and most of the regular petty officers, artificers and mechanicians were survivors who rightly felt they had done their bit. There was also an infusion of Barrack Stanchions, men who, thus far, had avoided sea service. As the war in Europe drew to a close they had now been rumbled and had no urge to do their bit anyway. Among the officers were four ex-Keyham, one highly experienced whose lugubrious expression concealed a rocklike calm for which I was to be grateful, the second his complete opposite. For all the latter's excitability he was a willing horse who drove himself too hard. The other two, like me, were new to the ship and finding their feet. There were also two keen but inexperienced RNVR officers and two superlative warrant engineers.

Commander (E) had been *Hood's* senior when I, as a midshipman, was fighting the decision to become an engineer. Tactfully he had gone on leave during what should have been my turnover from Walker. Our first meeting 24 hours after Walker's departure gave me the feeling that he now felt a bit professionally bereft and I didn't blame him. Nevertheless I sensed he would let me run things my own way provided my way worked. As he was in the promotion zone my neck would be on the block if things went wrong. Poor man! He quickly received a shock when an Admiralty signal arrived which read, *Dr Wilson, senior psychologist, is appointed Duke of York (temporarily) to study the actions of the senior engineer*. I found it hard to convince my chief that Dr Wilson was responsible for the entry standards of engineer officers. At Keyham I had challenged the yardsticks he was applying which to me stemmed from his ignorance of the life and work of seagoers. Though I had not been warned of it, the signal, I averred, was Wilson's revenge! Happily it was and another friendship was born when Dr Wilson took the trouble, on my behalf, to define the differences between psychiatry as an aid to the mentally deranged, and industrial psychology (his particular forte), a difference clearly not appreciated by the commander (E).

My chief backed overtime and would stop leave until the job was done whereas I preferred strict punctuality and, when setting tasks, relied on my judgement as to the time they might take. I rewrote the standing orders paraphrasing Commander Rory O'Conor's Ten Commandments. Two of these have always stuck in my mind: *Each man is personally responsible for his punctual attendance at his place of duty* which I recalled when some HO petty officers made it apparent they had differing views from mine as to the importance of that punctuality. O'Conor had also written, *You can afford to act calmly observing that your orders are backed by the authority of the whole Service, the Naval Discipline Act, with the Lords Spiritual and Temporal and all the Commons in support.* (E) officers have to learn early how to deal with indiscipline without immediate resort to the Naval Discipline Act and without the rancour which can so quickly result in sabotage below, where opportunity abounds. After one major confrontation with the newly arrived petty officers I had my way. The tedious work of storing for a campaign in which, like it or not we would all be involved, and where machinery failure due to slackness or sabotage would spell disaster for all, was accomplished in working hours.

We were greatly heartened by a visit from King George VI and Queen Elizabeth who, with that flair which has never deserted her, picked out the youngest stokers to speak to. As she said to me afterwards, *they look about 12.* They were in fact 16. The king also commended himself to the engineers when he pointed out to the gunnery officer that the roses on our gun tompions were painted red, Lancaster's colour, instead of white, York's. Soon after I was passed a letter from a worried mother who had not heard from young Harry and was afraid he might be getting into bad company. I was able to reassure her that Harry had not ventured ashore since joining and that the only lady he had spoken to was Her Majesty!

Thanks to the naval manpower shortage we were 15% short of stokers. Two days pre-sailing leave ensured that this figure rose to 20% for whom the drafting office had no reserves: naval prisons and detention centres had been cleared and the residents dispatched to the Pacific. We would catch up with a load in *HMS Effingham* in Colombo they told us. Until when we would have to lump it.

We raised steam at midnight for a dawn departure but a gale sprang up and the pilot felt unable to take us safely out of the Gladstone dock. By noon we had shut down the machinery and once more gave short leave which we did each afternoon for the three days the gale lasted, bad for machinery and crew. Steam joints started to leak, precious boiler hours were used up and the ship's company farewells became spectacularly alcoholic. On the fourth day the navigator, with whom I had become firm friends, warned me that heavy engine movements would be needed. In turn I asked him to warn the captain that this would mean much smoke as nearly a third of our stokers had never been to sea. Departure matched our predictions and an emergency full speed caused a thick black cloud to drift over Bootle. My chief, who had wisely remained above decks, felt constrained to acquaint me of this phenomenon in terms which suggested I should do something. In fact I had refrained from bothering the chief stoker concerned who would be as aware as anyone what was happening. However 'needs must'... but the reply I got over the phone surprised me.

Don't mind the f - - - - smoke, the f- - - - boiler room is flooding.

A young ordnance artificer had achieved the impossible and had so cross-connected valves on the hydraulic main operating the turrets that full hydraulic pressure was directed into a storage tank adjoining the boiler room. When this burst resoundingly, the fluid drained into the bilges. Once safely in Scapa Flow the depot ship helped us repair the now bulging bulkhead and the equally bulging and slightly split deck above the tank.

Shortly before sailing I had received a dividend from my recent Keyham days: three young officers persuaded the appointers to send them to *Duke of York* at the expense of their leave. In the trying days ahead I came to rely on Don Spiller, Mick Lyne and Jim Flower. Their rapid progress towards watchkeeping certificates proved how wise Captain Sebastian had been to insist on sending midshipmen (E) to sea where they had absorbed enough practical engineering to hold their own with the artificers and enhance their already considerable leadership qualities.

After a hectic work-up, much gunfire and, surprisingly, a successful full power trial that raised my rather lowly standing in my chief's eyes, we sailed for Malta with *Anson* who, like us, was desperately short of stokers and had received a similar response from the drafting authorities. We reached Malta in time for VE-Day. The patch above the damaged hydraulic tank in an electrical machinery space did not satisfy the electrical artificer concerned so he arranged a little private enterprise with a welder friend. Neither took the statutory fire precautions thus, inevitably, fire started. Both had the sense to remove the oxygen and acetylene bottles before evacuating the compartment and raising the alarm. I arrived to find dense smoke and an argument amongst a number of potential Casabiancas about who should wear the breathing apparatus which was quickly settled. The fire, I found, was easily extinguished. Unfortunately it had been near the ship's ring main whose insulation was found to be slightly affected. My chief and I agreed that the ship's programme need not be changed so 'press on' was our advice. Officially it was not our responsibility but, in those curious days, that of the torpedo officer, advised by the commissioned electrician. Against our advice they decided not to take the risk so *Anson* sailed a week ahead of us to reach Colombo and the reserves of stokers first, while we dallied for our ring main to be made perfect.

From Malta we passed over the spot where *Naiad* lay and then practised bombardment, which was to be our role in the Pacific, against western desert targets. And so to Port Said. *Anson* drew six inches less than us which gave her just a foot between her bottom and the largely undredged Suez canal. At the end of her passage she had signalled that her condensers were clogged with sand. Clearly ours would fare worse. At one point we stuck fast to Egypt, one propeller firmly embedded in Sinai as we tried in vain to answer the telegraph and go Full Astern - to the detriment of the gearing, as we found later. Eventually we won through past troopships in Lake Timsah full of cheerful soldiers shouting, *You're going the wrong way.* At Suez we had two hectic days digging out sand. Unlike *Hood's* problem in 1939, *Duke of York's* condensers were roomy and our enemy this time was heat, not cold. Our young men, now more willing, were understandably less stalwart than those with whom we had started the war. It had been bitterly cold in Liverpool and Scapa, but now heat exhaustion reared its head. I saw a signal from the light fleet carriers further down the Red Sea reporting the death from heatstroke of an exceptionally fit young Lieutenant (E) I had taught at Keyham. Clearly this was a danger.

We all wanted to catch up *Anson* but our speed down the Red Sea depended on how many boilers we could man. Optimistically we settled for 22 knots and six of our eight boilers. On the first night out of Suez a phone call in the early hours informed me that most of the engineering and seamen petty officers were suffering acute diarrhoea. This was difficult to understand as I had refused a waterboat at Suez because of a similar experience in *Naiad*. The surgeon commander was as great a believer in Dr Collis Browne's Chlorodyne as I: his powerful version quickly returned my people to duty in a comfortable haze of opium, but we had to find the cause or the whole ship might be struck down. It took only a few minutes to identify the offending water tank: a sample revealed a disgustingly smelly soapy solution. The filling funnel for that particular tank, into which the newly-made water from the evaporators discharged, was in the officers' lower cabin flat well below the waterline. The effluent from their individual washbasins was normally collected into copper receptacles of Nelsonic design by a marine employed to carry these slops up two vertical ladders and empty them into the officers' heads. Observing the adjacent filling funnel (wrongly left open) suggested that he should forego the weary climb and empty the copper cans into this obviously convenient receptacle, his practice since leaving Malta.

After ditching the dirty water we invited him to help the stokers clean the tank.

My experiences in *Naiad* led me to ask the executive commander whether part of the upper deck could be reserved for the engineering department to sunbathe, not to enhance their beauty (we knew nothing of skin cancer) but to brown their bodies and so reduce the agonies of prickly heat. In *Naiad* this had not been possible because we were always in action and had suffered accordingly. The commander readily agreed. Pre-war warship ventilation was disgracefully primitive and a blot on the constructors and civilian electrical engineers in the design departments, but at sea its operation was our department's responsibility. Despite organising wind tunnels and a better flow of air through the messdecks, prickly heat became a general scourge. Hence sunbathing for all was encouraged.

In the Red Sea the wind invariably seems to come from astern, so funnel gases were drawn along with the ship which added to our misery. Four liquids essential to keep the boiler and engine room crews on their feet were the excellent naval lime juice to prevent scurvy, hot tea to encourage sweating, oatmeal water said to prevent prickly heat and salty water to replace the salt sweated out and so obliterate cramps. Tea and salt were the vital items, but salt water is an emetic and stokers can be heavy-handed. In *Naiad* I had managed to buy sufficient tasteless salt tablets in Alexandria but our surgeon commander could procure none in England or Malta. Twenty-four hours after leaving Suez the heat, messdeck stench and the pervasive funnel gases started to take their toll; young stokers dropped like flies. At one moment on my rounds I found myself in charge of a steaming boiler room, assisted only by the chief stoker and petty officer water tender. We organised a burly and cheerful stoker petty officer and two older men to help or hoist the bodies to the airlocks, revive them and, depending on their state and personal guts, of which most had plenty, to return them to their boiler room or find a substitute. This is the sort of crisis which pulls an engine room department together and older stokers, with softer jobs as pantry hands and messmen, quickly volunteered to go below. I felt however that this was not the time to call on them, for if we wore out the older men too soon we should have no reserves when the real fighting started. Despite my chief's wishes, who thought I was letting the side down, I approached the marine major. Royal Marines and stokers have always got on together and I was aware that, as a relic of coal-burning days, there was a paragraph in *King's Regulations* permitting marines to be employed and paid as stokers. There was a spate of volunteers who quickly picked up the job of swopping and cleaning oil fuel sprayers and the routines of steady steaming. By the time we reached Colombo most of the stokers had found their feet and resumed their duties, the marines gloating over their inflated pay packets.

Eight days in Colombo gave us time to swop experiences with *Anson* before she left. We also 'welcomed' stokers from HMS *Effingham*, not all prisoners or deserters. *Anson* had treated us very fairly when she had had first pick.

Indeed I was glad to spot a few stalwarts I had served with before but outwardly the remainder were unprepossessing; mostly scouses from Liverpool with chips on their shoulders at being

Pacific-bound. Fortunately I was backed by good officers. My senior chief stoker, though apt to panic, would always warn me of trouble in the offing. The department, recovering quickly from our Red Sea ordeal, seemed well on the way to becoming an effective team but the ex-gaolbirds had to be watched. In machinery spaces and badly ventilated messdecks feelings in the tropics always run high so that an ill-considered remark, a blow threatened or delivered, can waste time at the defaulter's table and cause lasting ill will. I took care, daily, to tell the stokers on the messdecks at dinner time the latest war news and ship's plans. Disinformation is the weapon of trouble-makers and this we prevented. On our last sunday in Colombo and in honour of a distinguished visitor the captain decided to have full divisions which hindered refitting and created a stupendous messdeck moan. Stokers especially hate divisions. As we had some Welsh stokers with melodious voices and the bandmaster was an old friend from my midshipman's days in *Hood,* I secretly arranged that on marching off our two stoker divisions, assisted by the band, would leave the quarterdeck singing, *Yo ho, yo ho and off to work we go,* which they did, fortissimo, to the delight of the visiting potentate.

On arrival in Perth a signal was received ordering me to fly ahead of the ship to Sydney where I was whisked to the fleet engineer's offices. Here the fleet staff's dilemma was explained. *HMS King George V* with my old Keyham Commander, Gerry Cook, as chief and flying the flag of Vice Admiral Sir Bernard Rawlings, (who had saved *Naiad's* bacon at Crete) had recently completed two operations with the American fleet in the forward area lasting three and four weeks respectively. The bombardment of Sakashima Gunto by *King George V, Howe* and the British carriers had neutralised Japanese air support from Formosa to Okinawa then under fierce American attack. *Howe* was now non-operational and returning to UK. As *King George V's* fighting effectiveness was also seriously in doubt, *Duke of York* was scheduled to take her place. Against this *Duke of York* had been at sea for 60 out of the last 90 days. It was months since she had been docked for a bottom scrape, her officers had no Pacific operational experience and, more importantly, no knowledge of US Navy operational and communication procedures. Admiral Rawlings felt that we might prove more of an encumbrance than an asset if dispatched immediately. Mechanically, I reported, *Duke of York* was in good state and if we could use US navy boiler compound then our boiler hours could be extended and we would have plenty in hand. Thus did I fall into a trap. *Just what we wanted to hear*, said the fleet engineer officer.

Unwittingly I had confirmed his view that *Duke of York* should be cannibalised to provide spares for *King George V*, so a signal went off ordering vital generators and air compressors to be stripped for transfer to *King George V* immediately *Duke of York* arrived in Sydney. I was then dispatched to *King George V* to tell Commander Cook what was afoot. I was shocked to see him and his officers: all looked old men. Their experiences had revealed the inadequacies of the design of British warships whose mobility was pathetic compared with the US Navy's.

When the *Duke of York* arrived my reception was noticeably cool, but my explanations were reinforced by the arrival both of the fleet engineer officer and Admiral Fraser who had come to welcome his old flagship from Home Fleet days. Working parties were quickly sent to *King George V* to instal our machinery and help her weary engineers make her as operationally serviceable as possible. Then she sailed once more with Admiral Rawlings to become part of Admiral 'Bull' Halsey's task force. *Duke of York* and her ship's company were left to hang about Wooloomooloo, Garden Island dockyard and the erotic delights of Sydney until *King George V's* spares arrived by air from UK and we could fit them.

Although *Duke of York* was never to fire again in anger we left Sydney expecting to fight. After reaching Manus, the British Pacific fleet's advance base, Admiral Fraser came on board and hoisted his flag as Commander-in-Chief, British Pacific Fleet. On our way to Guam rumours spread that some incredible new bomb had been dropped on the Japanese as indeed, on the day we arrived, was a second. At Guam Admiral Fraser invested Admiral Chester Nimitz USN with the Grand Cross of the Order of the Bath which gave us the chance to meet that great man with his ice blue eyes. While guests of his staff on a local beach - with Japanese soldiers still known to be in the adjoining undergrowth - we learned that the enemy had sued for peace.

We were at sea on VJ-Day, August 15, recovering from a typhoon. Joining Halsey's third fleet a little later and determined to show our prowess, we approached his flagship at 25 knots when our rudder jammed. We roared through his fleet with two

• *After the Duke of York had spliced the main brace Admiral 'Bull' Halsey USN came over by jackstay transfer to check the rum's quality. His ships, then as now, were 'dry'*

black not-under-control balls at the yardarm.

Welcome. A most spectacular arrival, was Halsey's greeting. Later came a signal from King George telling us to splice the main brace followed by another from Halsey with the same message, *Negative all US task forces.* A week later we entered Tokyo Bay in company with *King George V*, never our 'chummy' ship. Although Admiral Rawlings was not the C-in-C Fraser, in a typical gesture, though flying his flag in *Duke of York*, had placed her under Rawlings' operational command. The latter was therefore within his rights when he signalled us, *It is usual to remove tompions when action is likely.* This caused enormous offence in the executive world. Tompions were not in the gun muzzles but, in accordance with Home Fleet practice and because of the recent typhoon, there were canvas covers over the muzzles to keep out damp and spray. Shortly after we anchored I received a note from Commander (E) Cook saying how deeply grateful *King George V* was for our cannibalised machinery which had worked perfectly and for the help we had given in Sydney; and would I care to bring over a team of (E) officers for a drink, a typically graceful gesture. But it was clear, when we got there that, engineers apart, we were unwelcome. My opposite number was ill in his cabin and Cook was clearly on the verge of collapse from heat and fatigue. Shortly afterwards he was flown home but received no recognition for keeping Rawlings' flagship serviceable.

In Tokyo Bay, Admiral Sir Bruce Fraser as C-in-C and *Duke of York*, his flagship, were given the place of honour next to the great *USS Missouri* where the surrender of Japan was to take place. We still carried a beautiful admiral's barge which, as there was nothing like it in the US fleet, Fraser loaned together with its superlatively smart crew, all on their mettle. Nimitz was delighted and used it continuously for his various official visits. Next came a request from the *Missouri* to borrow our wooden wardroom chairs, thought to be more suitable for the great to sit on at the surrender table than the *Missouri's* utilitarian steel ones.

The evening before the surrender, a posse of the British press arrived on board including the famous Stanley Maxted and David Divine. By now, after a month at sea, we were acutely short of water to the extent that I broadcast the amount remaining every four hours. I had not gone as far as a contemporary who drilled holes in the wardroom baths an inch from the bottom until defeated by his surgeon commander who arrived with corks. But I had painted lines an inch from the bottom of each bath and, when that looked like failing, I locked the bathrooms except for a few set hours a day, and kept the key. My surrender day started about 0500 when a gaggle of furious pressmen burst into my cabin and demanded the bathroom key to shave before being ferried over to the *Missouri*. The small round man in a purple rage leading the assault was David Divine. From that unsatisfactory start a friendship developed with that most patriotic and articulate naval correspondent which I have greatly treasured.

Sadly only a small contingent of British and Commonwealth ships were present. As our tankers were both slow and few, there were insufficient available to support more than a microcosm of the large British Pacific fleet. Only two battleships, the carrier *Indefatigable*, some cruisers, destroyers and a small part of the fleet train witnessed the end of the war. From our front row of the stalls we watched the arrival of Admiral Nimitz, General MacArthur, Admiral Fraser and other allied representatives as well as Chinese and Soviet delegates. Then came foreign minister Shigemitsu in formal morning dress and black top hat, accompanied by a uniformed General Umezu. As the Japanese were leaving after the ceremony it was discovered that one allied

• *Awaiting sunset aboard HMS Duke of York, September 2, 1945*

representative had signed on the wrong line and so amendments had to be made.

The surrender and succeeding jubilation was rightly American but, as Admiral Fraser appreciated, Britain and the Commonwealth had now been at war for six long years less a day. If the forenoon had been American then the evening would be British. The last sunset ceremony had been carried out on the evening of September 2, 1939. Since then the white ensign had flown in every ship by day and night. Admiral Fraser ordered the resumption of sunset routine as from September 2, 1945 and invited all the senior officers of British ships in Tokyo and a token number of sailors from each, to witness the ceremony in his flagship. He was dissuaded from firing a sunset gun in case some trigger-happy American or Japanese thought the war had re-started.

Only Captain Roy Dowling RAN, my old *Naiad* commander and now the senior Australian afloat, refused. His commander signalled that Dowling had collapsed with glandular fever or dengue. In some extraordinary way Fraser knew that Dowling and I had served together and also that the latter was likely, as he did, to rise to the top of his own navy, so he felt it essential that Dowling should be present if humanly possible. I was therefore bundled into the c-in-c's temporary barge with a bottle of champagne and told to dose Dowling and get him on his feet or, if he was too ill, to leave the champagne for later with the commander-in-chief's compliments. Dowling had not been told of the invitation, but against the advice of his surgeon commander, and fortified with the champagne, his old humour reasserted itself and we manhandled him on board *Duke of York*.

Allied and Commonwealth flags were flying from the fore and main yardarms with the commander-in-chief's flag at the masthead and the white ensign at the gaff. On X and Y turrets and the after superstructure there was a great river of khaki-clad figures, to the extent that with all the unaccustomed topweight *Duke of York* developed a slight loll against the background of Fujiyama's snow-tipped peak, turning pink as the sun dropped to the horizon.

Roy Dowling's bottle of champagne was not the only one cracked that evening and sunset had to be postponed while our guests carefully climbed up to the quarterdeck. When Admiral Fraser arrived the quartermaster reported, *Sunset, sir*. The still sounded. The Royal Marine guard presented arms and the band played, *The day Thou gavest Lord is ended*, interspersed with the sunset call as only Royal Marine buglers know how. For the first time in six bitter years the white ensign came down. Many, perhaps most, had never before savoured the magic of this moment when the busy life of a warship is hushed and the evening comes. Others of us, standing at the salute, were in tears as we remembered those who would never again see colours in the morning or hear the bugles sound sunset at dusk. I thought of all those friends in *Hood* who had come to see me off and the many many others; and in *Naiad* of old Stoker Petty Officer West lying on the floor of my cabin, his damage control section HQ, bleeding from a terrible wound and saying, as we lifted him onto my bunk, *I've picked up a little puncture, sir. I don't want to mess up your blankets*; of little Stoker Storey arriving at the bottom of the engine room ladder with the teaboat as the torpedo came in; of Stoker Harrison, alone in his dynamo room without the companion who had been with him at action stations, and with no escape to the upper deck; of old Lambkin, immured in his steel box with the steering gear. Had he been let out or had he died as *Naiad* slid stern first to the sea floor?

As the white ensign came into the hands of our chief yeoman and the carry-on sounded, we realised that on board all the great US ships around us every activity had stopped, their sailors facing towards the British flagship and saluting us. Perhaps the special relationship between our two countries was born that evening.

CHAPTER 12

From war to peace

At the first of the Anglo-American conferences, Admiral Nimitz enquired about the sea-keeping capacity of the British fleet. He was told that the fleet had not mastered the swift underway-refuelling techniques used by the Americans. As he afterwards told the story, 'Admiral Fraser and I had a long conference . . . He felt he could operate for eight days a month, and we compromised on 20.'

Nimitz, Professor E B Potter, Naval Institute Press

SHORTLY BEFORE *DUKE OF YORK* finally left Sydney my chief developed a cheshire cat grin which even our spectacular arrival with the US Third Fleet barely disturbed. His relief was due and, in fact, arrived the day after the surrender. My new chief had no wartime sea experience and had been heavily indoctrinated by Bath's reactionary hierarchy as to the mutinous attitude of Pacific fleet engineers. What particularly angered HQ was the continuing use, against specific orders, of a chemical known as US boiler compound which enabled the fleet to treble the hours between boiler cleaning without damage to the boilers.

Although chemical treatment of boiler water to prevent internal corrosion of boilers had long been adopted by the British power station industry and was used most satisfactorily in the US destroyers given to Britain and later in US warships working with the Home Fleet, the technical view of senior officers in the engineer-in-chief's department at Bath and at the Admiralty Fuel Experiment Station was wholly against this innovation for two reasons of which only one was technical. They believed (wrongly) that 'priming' (the carrying over of water droplets in the steam from the highly forced naval boilers) would occur, which would damage turbines and machinery: and secondly and almost unbelievably that boiler cleaning at intervals of only 750 hours (instead of with chemical treatment at 2000-hour intervals) was essential to give crews a rest; and this despite the desperate shortage of operational escorts everywhere and that the boiler cleaners would, in most cases, be the most hard worked part of the ship's company anyway. A documented and photographed in-service trial in *HMS Victorious* on passage to the Pacific - carried out against specific orders from Bath - by Lieutenant Commander (E) Leonard Baker DSC her senior engineer (who had just come from the boiler specialist section at Bath) with the approval of his chief, Commander (E) Basil Cronk DSC, and his captain (later Admiral Sir Michael Denny) proved conclusively that no priming occurred. In fact the trial boilers with chemical treatment were in better condition after 2000 hours than untreated boilers after 750 hours. As a result of *Victorious'* trial and its potential operational benefit Denny reported the matter to Admiral Vian, commanding the carriers. Very quickly permission was given by Vice-Admiral Charles Daniel in Sydney for all British Pacific ships to use chemical treatment in evaporators and boilers and extend the boiler cleaning interval to 2000 hours. The chemical itself was freely available from USN sources.

On his return to UK Baker, who likes to be called an innovator rather than a rebel or revolutionary, was threatened with court martial by Bath's engineering hierarchy but Admiralty did not endorse this. Historically Baker's action may be likened to that of Commander Henderson, a member of the naval staff in world war one and later Controller of the Navy. In leaking the truth to the secretary of the cabinet about the number of ocean-going ships requiring convoy protection Henderson triggered the move towards convoys just in time to save Britain's defeat by starvation. Without Baker's action the British Pacific Fleet's contribution would have been miniscule. Baker later chose to retire from the navy after contributing greatly to the future of gas turbines in warships, to become marine superintendent of the Blue Funnel Line.

I managed to establish a happy relationship with my old chief who understood both our shortage of drinking water and the difficulties of keeping pace with the boiler water consumption due to steam leaks. Our 30 tropical days at sea since Sydney, including a typhoon, had accentuated these shortages of which I had been warned. Further our bursts of high speed steaming in the high water temperatures of the Pacific meant that the boilers had to reach maximum forcing rate to produce enough steam for the speeds demanded. The water-contaminated oil fuel from our rickety tankers damaged our furnace brickwork and my chief agreed that the *Engineering Manual* rules were wholly inappropriate to Pacific conditions. If I had become a rather emotional engineering revolutionary, he was not far off. As soon as we anchored in Tokyo bay we reverted to four hours' notice for steam on our main engines. This meant we could start to take apart leaky steam pipe joints from which so much precious boiler feed water was lost and so much heat engendered, and substitute the more satisfactory US-type jointing material I had acquired in Sydney. Brave men in wet fearnought suits repaired fallen brickwork in boiler furnaces that were still hot. With peace it was possible, too, to rig upper deck salt-water showers which saved distilled water. This work strained an engineering department already worn by watchkeeping in the appalling heat below.

Our sickness rate among the young stokers and some of the older skilled hands rose and the (E) officers, even though we had not been in action, felt the strain. One faithful zealot, suffering from a nervous skin complaint, had to be flown back to Sydney; another, for whom I had little sympathy, immured himself in his cabin alleging chest pains until our tough Irish doctor evicted him. But the stalwart three who had joined us shortly before leaving Liverpool, now qualified watchkeepers, were a welcome and always cheerful reinforcement. The RNVR officers went from strength to strength but the two older warrant engineers were nearing the end of their tether. Recalling my *Hood* experience I made one of the newly qualified lieutenants (E) responsible for the boiler rooms, where the worst conditions prevailed, to lighten the load on the warrant engineers whose long experience was so valuable to me and spread the rest of the duties amongst the remainder. Before he left my old chief warned me that his successor was a 'by the book' man and that I would be meeting problems.

My new chief was charming but his engineering philosophy was attuned to the *Engineering Manual* and Bath's handed-down tablets of wholly inappropriate wisdom which we had abandoned for reasons already given. Most of *Duke of York's* boilers had steamed for more than 750 hours so, by the book, should be cleaned. But few approached the 2000 hours which the use of US Navy chemical water treatment, forbidden by Bath, safely allowed. It is easy to argue with someone dislikeable but less so with someone to whom one is drawn. His instructions were clear: no more steam pipes to be dismantled, installation of salt water showers on the upper deck curtailed and the two boilers with the most steaming hours to be opened up for his inspection. Brickwork repairs, he conceded reluctantly, could continue. Explaining this to my hardworked men was not easy but we calculated the chief would be able to inspect a group of boilers within 48 hours with which he would have to be content.

Next day Commander Cook in the *King George V* collapsed and was flown to the UK. His senior, too, was out of action. Like *Duke of York*, *King George V* was ostensibly at four hours' notice for steam but, emergency apart, it would take at least that time to get her under way. Someone had to replace Cook and quickly. With the agreement of Admiral Rawlings my new chief was appointed to *King George V* and left us within a couple of hours. Given the acting rank of Commander (E) I was now fully responsible and quickly reverted to the previous refitting arrangements which state of affairs lasted all of three days. Clearly *King George V* would have to return to UK but it would be unfair to other officers longer on the station if my new chief went with her so he returned to *Duke of York!* During my short interregnum two things had happened. First the commander-in-chief told me to give him my own and contemporaries' views, (*worm's eye view* he described it) as to why the operational capacity, mobility in particular, of the British ships was so manifestly inferior to that of the US fleet, a report that was to go directly to *Duke of York's* Captain Nicholl, Fraser's flag captain, rather than through engineering channels. The second event was that my new chief returned a changed man. As St Paul's eyes were opened on the road to Damascus so were Commander (E) Toby Hindson's during his brief but obviously shattering three days in *King George V*. And only someone of his moral stature could have seen the light so clearly in the face of the working-over he had received before leaving the UK. I confessed that I had over-ruled his previous orders but, to my delight, he enthusiastically endorsed my action. He also offered to help me with the report demanded by the commander-in-chief and with his wide Admiralty experience this was invaluable. Then he instructed me to visit *King George V* , *Indefatigable* and the *USS Missouri* for evidence.

Four factors influenced the writing of that report. First my Pacific-experienced contemporaries had to understand this was not an inquest into how they ran their machinery but a genuine enquiry by the commander-in-chief who had been controller of the navy and thus in charge of all materiel matters. Secondly, conclusions drawn would be general with no particular ships quoted. Thirdly, my report which certainly would be critical of the design departments in Bath must therefore be strictly factual rather than anecdotal. Fourthly, I had to provide lessons from the US navy. The *Missouri* had already been more than 90 days continuously at sea and in action for much of the time, yet the US fleet was still at only 30 minutes notice for steam (as opposed to our rather shaky four hours) and apparently ready for an equally prolonged period at sea in action. How was this achieved? Alas I have no copy of my report which had to be typed by a coder as it would have leaked if done in the engineer's office; nor, more recently, can I find it in the Public Record Office. I hoped that by painting as vivid a picture as I was able of Pacific engineering operational conditions the revolutionary designers in Bath might be provided with evidence to enable them to work even more effectively for a return to unrestricted mobility. Of course the *King George V* class design had been constrained by cost and limiting naval treaties between the wars whereas the much larger *Missouri* had been built regardless of expense and with the benefits of advanced technology. But that excuse could go only so far.

Because I have been unable to obtain a copy of my report, I wrote to Captain R G McClement whom I had taught at Keyham. He was a survivor from *HMS Penelope* and an experienced watch-keeper in *HMS King George V* in the Pacific. The five main problem areas he lists coincide with my recollection.

Furnace brickwork Due to the Pacific seawater temperature of 90°F *King George V* could not maintain full vacuum in her condensers designed for more temperate oceans. When operating with fast carriers the boilers were always at maximum output for long periods to enable the battleship to keep up. As the aged fleet train tankers were apt to supply oil fuel contaminated with seawater this, combined with prolonged high furnace temperatures, damaged the latter's brickwork. Relays of the few skilled bricklayers, led by an officer, had to enter the hot furnaces wrapped in wet asbestos suits for ten-minute spells, less if they collapsed.

Superheaters *Duke of York* had suffered minor leaks in her superheater header tube joints which caused boiler feed water losses, but *King George V* had been plagued with major leaks since the refit.   Finally, just before *King George V's* first operation, Commander Cook threw the *Engineering Manual* out of the scuttle and injected manganesite between tube ends and headers.   Only two of the engineering department, Lieutenant (E) A O Gaunt and a chief engine room artificer, were small enough to get into the 16 superheater headers and for months afterwards both suffered appalling skin troubles.   The chief artificer was awarded the Distinguished Service Medal.   Gaunt was later invalided.   The resultant reduction in feed water losses made it possible (just) for *King George V* to remain at sea.

Leaking steam pipe joints and glands Captain McClement, as a senior Lieutenant (E), swapped duties with his opposite number, the senior watchkeeper in *Missouri,* and found it difficult to realise that the US ship was steam-driven.   The US officer in *King George V,* on the other hand, claimed his time on board the British ship was the nearest thing to hell he had experienced as most of the steam seemed to be outside the pipes.   Here McClement's experience coincides precisely with mine when in my normal white uniform I toured *Missouri's* machinery compartments without sweating at a period when she was at 30 minutes' notice for sea after 92 consecutive days under way.   The *Missouri's* senior engineer, equipped by me with overalls over a pair of rugger shorts, begged off when I had taken him only a quarter of my forenoon rounds.

Perpetual water shortages With her superheater headers more or less cured, if unconventionally, *King George V* was still desperately short of water.   One set of evaporators continuously distilled boiler feed water, the other set for half the time.   Drinking/ washing water had to be rationed on an hour-to-hour basis, an intolerable hardship for a ship's company at action stations.   The emergency evaporators, hopefully fitted to all the class before leaving the UK, discharged directly into the main condensers; any operational mistake causing impure water at once contaminated the whole boiler water supply in a single main machinery unit, a quite impermissible risk.   They were therefore useless.

In one respect only did *Duke of York,* new on the station, manage to surpass the troubles of *King George V, Howe* or *Anson* and most other ships in the Pacific.   Put simply an evaporator is like an electric kettle except that the water heating is done by pipes carrying hot steam and not an element carrying an electric current. The steam is led away to a distiller while the salt remains coated on the steam coils. The distiller, a honeycomb of tubes through which passes sea water, condenses the steam from the evaporator leaving a condensate which should be pure distilled water. *Duke of York's* distillers were supposed to have been re-tubed during the refit but suddenly and within minutes of each other, exactly 2000 miles from Tokyo and the same distance from Sydney, both distillers started leaking salt water into the distilled water used by the boilers and for drinking purposes. Thoughtless designers, pressed for space under treaty limits, had located the distillers in the hottest and least accessible corner of the machinery room where the temperature was 110°F plus. When, eventually, we dismantled them we discovered supervision had been lacking and only half the tubes in each distiller had been renewed. Working in shifts under Mechanician Vosper, on whose shoulders our whole water supply had for so long rested, we managed to fit spare tubes to one distiller to produce good boiler water. The other we managed to repair only sufficiently to produce water for drinking but not up to boiler standard. At the height of the crisis, with both evaporators out of action, we were within an hour of running out of water altogether. Had we been at war a major catastrophe would have ensued.

Main machinery design British boiler, turbine and gearing designs were so behind the US navy's that our miles-per-gallon were far worse. This meant more frequent fuelling at sea and more broken fuelling hoses because we were neither sufficiently skilled nor fitted for this evolution (a steady supply of new hoses had to be flown out from the UK and up to Manus by the RAF). As we took longer for each fuelling and ammunition replenishment, more high speed steaming was needed to keep up with the Americans. Had we not used the forbidden boiler compound British warships would have had to withdraw for unnecessary boiler cleaning and there would have been little or none of the BPF left mobile.

Either in this or in a subsequent report I made further points. Messdeck ventilation was so ill-thought out and primitive that no man could give of his best in the conditions to which he was condemned. Secondly the war had added vast amounts of new equipment not catered for in the ship's initial design - laundries for example. Finally peacetime designs had failed to foresee the extra numbers required for war, so sanitary arrangements were insufficient. The armoured decks of our carriers were far more effective against damage than the US wooden decks: that apart it was clear that many US ships, thanks to well-conceived damage control provisions, had absorbed damage that would have sunk British ships.

At first our carriers' machinery seemed in better state than our battleships' but after talking to my opposite numbers I concluded that this was marginal because they were newer designs and had greater horsepower to call on, although their messdeck ventilation was as appalling as the battleships'. The vibration in *Howe* and *King George V*, during their short periods (compared to US ships) of intensive bombardment with 14in salvos, badly affected steam joints and increased the need for machinery maintenance. My visits to US ships also persuaded me that USN deck officers were more technically minded than their RN equivalents and the few Engineering Duties Only (EDO) officers they carried were far-sighted and sophisticated engineers. But this certainly did not apply to their enlisted men: my rather brash conclusion was that the US navy achieved its superb mobility through sophisticated design, resulting in ships easy to maintain and operate, even with the lower standard of enlisted men. British ships in the Pacific had achieved miracles of mobility, although far below the Americans, despite out-dated, inefficient ship and machinery design, because of the professional training and leadership of our long-service ratings and officers.

My report was such an emotional and outspoken document that a newly-arrived senior staff engineer, lacking Pacific experience, pressured me with a good lunch to withdraw it in my own interests as it so ruthlessly criticised the Bath design departments. However, enthusiastically received by Admiral Fraser's staff, it was already on its way to London. On the voyage home and at their suggestion and with my chief's help, I put together another report on the selection, structure and training of future engineering personnel.

These two rather amateurish reports were to shape my future naval career.

From Tokyo *Duke of York* hurried towards Hong Kong for the Japanese surrender on September 16, 1945. By the time we arrived Admiral Harcourt had led in the relieving forces and was designated acting governor. Our task was to disarm the Japanese and restore the water, electricity and communications to some degree of normality. Our friends in *Anson* had already landed a sizeable body of men who were soon to be joined by *Duke of York's* Royal Marines, large numbers of sailors, quite a few stokers and some artificers to help in the power station. Lieutenants (E) with essential machinery responsibilities took over (executive) officer of the day responsibilities for running the whole ship's routine under the duty commanding officer.

My chief and I viewed these arrangements with mixed feelings. Men ashore meant delaying the ship's constant refitting work, but the landing also of lieutenants (E) in military command of sailors and stokers was a welcome innovation. Several ex-internees and prisoners of war, little better than skeletons who could hardly have survived another few weeks, came on board for a while. For them the war had finished only just in time.

With a new British government the colony's re-occupation had not been politically easy. General MacArthur had insisted that no allied landings should take place in his area before the formal surrender in Tokyo, yet everyone knew prisoners were dying daily. More difficult, General Chiang Kai-Shek wished to send two divisions through Hong Kong to occupy Canton further up the Yellow River. The British government assumed that the Americans would not stand in Chiang's way if he chose also to occupy Hong Kong. In these circumstances Fraser had to risk sending Harcourt into the colony with only *Euryalus* and the AA ship *Prince Robert*. More powerful forces were to follow later. Nevertheless all went well.

On arrival in Hong Kong Fraser felt it essential to call on the divisional general in Canton to acknowledge, on Britain's behalf, the way matters had been conducted. So he borrowed two RAF crash boats to take him, some of his staff and a small marine escort up river, and I was invited to join. Although my absence would add to my chief's already heavy load, there was some story that I needed a rest - or they needed one from me. We spent an interesting 36 hours in Canton, sleeping in the old and rather ghostly British Legation. Our hosts were attentive, providing a bottle of genuine Johnnie Walker (Black Label), between each host and dinner guest; and many toasts were drunk. After dinner we were invited to watch the execution of a number of collaborators which we politely declined. Instead, we pursued a somewhat erratic course back to the legation through streets still full of disarmed Japanese soldiers. Although we had a small Chinese military escort, we ourselves were unarmed. Eerie.

For the next 10 months we roamed the Pacific from Sydney to Japan, often via Hong Kong now rapidly returning to life. Personnel problems did not ease. More and more ratings were demobbed, their reliefs younger and greener. Most of our bad hats deserted in Australia where presumably they still are though none has yet featured in *Whicker's World*. My regulating chief stoker, now more experienced, was joined by one of *Naiad's* best petty officers by this time, deservedly, a chief stoker. So on practical engineering, rather than discipline, our worries concentrated. In training (for a marine engineering training ship was what we were becoming) I was brilliantly supported by the ex-Keyham and RNVR officers. The young artificers and even younger stokers, on their return from policing duties in Hong Kong, responded magnificently as we tailored our talks and practical instruction to what might also be useful to them in civilian life, as well as teaching them how to keep the ship mobile.

The next task was to transfer the BPF headquarters from Sydney to Hong Kong. On arrival at Wooloomooloo we approached too fast and, despite an emergency full astern, we penetrated some way into mainland Australia, damaging the gearing on one shaft as we were shortly to discover. Now that the war was over the older of our two warrant engineers decided to inspect the gears. We all thought it time to make a bow towards the normally discarded *Engineering Manual*. When the casing of the starboard outer gearbox was removed we could see that a six-inch chunk was missing from one pinion. Because the pieces had gone through the gearing there was other, though less serious, damage. Metallurgical examination at the Australian naval laboratory revealed that the final fracture had occurred in three stages: the first well over a year before, the second perhaps six months before and the third recently. From the pattern of fracture it was possible to say that each stage had occurred when the engines were going astern. Reference to the *Engineering Register* revealed that some tricky astern trials had taken place about 15 months before, personally supervised by the officer who was now deputy engineer-in-chief!

The second stage coincided with our passage through the Suez canal when this particular shaft had stuck in the mud as full astern steam was applied. The third obviously coincided with our recent encounter with the Australian mainland. We returned on three shafts to Hong Kong where we removed the heavy pinion with some rather shaky Japanese lifting gear, cleaned up the rough edges, lowered it again (vertically) through the hatch, brought it to the horizontal position and closed up the casing. With fingers crossed we gave ourselves a four-shaft 12 hour run at 80% full power, and all was well.

Our departure from Manila was also dramatic. There were a thousand wrecks in the harbour and the US navy told us precisely where we should anchor to avoid them which, as precisely, we did. Next morning the wind changed and the 200 or so ships in the harbour swung to it - except *Duke of York*.

You Brits always have to be different, was the comment of our US liaison officer. I put on a diving suit for the first time since my sub-lieutenant days and went down with a more experienced diver. We had anchored directly on top of the thousand and first wreck! Next day, in a rather tricky manoeuvre, we ground our way off without damaging our propellers but a sudden gush of oil from a fuel tank breathing pipe revealed, after another diver's examination, a four-foot gash in our bottom. The nearest available dry dock was Durban - where the girl I hoped to marry was serving as a Wren, but an unromantic Admiralty bade us carry on without using the damaged fuel tank.

At Kure we met the RFA amenities ship *Menestheus*. Although the cry from our ship's company of *Where are the dancing girls?* could not actually be satisfied, *Menestheus* had everything else: an all male concert party, cinema, shopping centre (with a Gieves), a restaurant with unlimited eggs, sausages, beans, fish and chips, and its own brewery with a lieutenant-commander master brewer and a 10 inch beer main which passed behind the ecumenical chapel's altar. The Americans had seen nothing like it and as the BPF was dwindling fast offered to buy *Menestheus*. Despite c-in-c's strong support, Whitehall refused.

I cannot recall how many bottles of whisky I had to pay for the amphibious jeep I acquired from the ever friendly, ever thirsty Americans. In it I visited the Imperial Japanese Naval Academy at Eta Jima which, architecturally, was a pocket edition of Dartmouth and, as I have read, with the same sadistic routines. Although already looted there were some well-made marine engineering models which I liberated and gave to Manadon on our return. On the fortieth anniversary of the end of the war with Japan, the Manadon captain, formerly British naval attaché in Tokyo, returned them to the Japanese attaché in London, a much appreciated gesture. *Duke of York's* gunroom was a good one and always up to some devilment for which often they suffered painfully. At Kure, by night, they scaled the masts of all the sunken Japanese ships and secured white ensigns to the mastheads. This was definitely a blow to any Special Relationship and the US navy were not amused; but no one seemed able to reach them and the offending white ensigns were still flying when we left.

At Kure of course the main interest was Hiroshima, not as devastated as Tokyo but probably with worse casualties. It was still possible to pick up water jugs which had melted in the heat, flattened by the blast and then reset. At Nagasaki which we visited shortly afterwards, great vertical steel pillars of factories had melted momentarily, been pushed over to 45° or so by blast and then rehardened. Here there had been a prisoner-of-war camp and we had reverently to bury the bones and skulls still sadly lying about. Nagasaki sickened us although it, too, seemed less damaged than Tokyo. Certainly, the new bomb saved the lives of hundreds of thousands of Americans, British and Japanese. Without at the time understanding what this device would come to mean to the world we regarded it with considerable satisfaction.

After these sombre visits we were sent to the island of Kagoshima to rest the sailors and permit a badly needed 'paint ship'.

As the first coat on the worst scars was applied, the local volcano, rather unfairly, chose to erupt. When he saw what the volcanic dust was doing to the paintwork our normally unflappable commander staged an eruption of his own. Our reactions below were equally hostile as the hard pumice dust penetrated our machinery. In high dudgeon *Duke of York* raised steam and left to encounter a major tidal wave en route to the open sea.

Christmas, when the navy still piped 'up spirits' at noon, was never an easy time for senior engineers. And the first post-war Christmas was no exception. After 'sippers' with each mess how Admiral Fraser, that most popular of admirals, remained upright I shall never know. In order to restore some semblance of sobriety to the engineering department the younger (E) officers challenged a petty officers' crew and stoker's crews to race around the ship in whalers. The sweat engendered gave hope that the evening might be peaceful but it was not to be. Our beloved commander-in-chief invited all the officers and chief and petty officers to drink with him on the quarterdeck. Typically generous as this gesture was it relit all the fires the whaler race had partially extinguished. However three other (E) officers split the night with me to ensure our machinery watchkeepers were still awake - and watching!

Shortly after Christmas the officers of a US cruiser came on board and were a little surprised to find our Captain, Angus Nicholl, famous for his leadership and brilliantly earned DSO in *HMS Penelope (Pepper Pot)* in Malta, not only joined in the fun but sat down at the piano and led us in song. That was always his way and we loved him for it. As US ships are dry the *USS Los Angeles* laid on a return party at Kowloon. We gathered at the Peninsular Hotel, tongues hanging out, until grinning Chinese waiters pulled back a curtain. Before us on the table was a Union Jack in red (rum), white (gin) and blue (gin coloured with ink, or so it tasted). Afterwards I was taken by our own artificers to a drinking den they had made their own. In my cabin next morning I found a certificate on my desk permitting me free drinks at this particular pub whenever I should call. I took it with me on a visit to Hong Kong 25 years later but the Hong Kong police did not consider it an entirely appropriate rendezvous for a director general of intelligence. Later I gave it to my son-in-law when his regiment was based there. By then alas the pub had gone.

Our trip home from Hong Kong via Singapore, Colombo and Malta was a triumphal tour for our commander-in-chief, now Lord Fraser of North Cape, carrying on the tradition of commemorating great naval victories. In Fraser's case this had been the sinking of the *Scharnhorst* while flying his flag in *Duke of York* so we were doubly pleased he was on board. At Plymouth we all expected that Fraser would be met by a member of the Board of Admiralty, or that we should hear that he was to be the next first sea lord, as Winston had offered when Dudley Pound died. But there was no one to welcome him. The ship's company determined to make up for this lack of recognition: the massive cheers came from our hearts as he went over the side.

If the *Duke of York* had been forgotten by the Admiralty, we were still remembered at Windsor. We received a welcoming signal from King George and Queen Elizabeth, who had come to say farewell at Liverpool, and they asked also if the Sea Ranger training ship at Windsor, of which the royal family were crew members, might be renamed *SRS Duke of York*. A week or so later we discovered that the *SRS Duke of York's* crew, including their royal highnesses, were camped in motor torpedo boats (whose decks they had to holystone) in the River Dart. This was an opportunity we could not miss. My old Dartmoor contacts provided plenty of Devonshire cream and strawberries to which we added sugar, still heavily rationed in the UK, but bought in Australia, with which we helped entertain them.

CHAPTER 13

From sea to shore

The profession of arms is an essential institution offering an orderly way of life, set a little apart, not without elegance . . . It will remain with us as long as man continues to be what he is, too clever and not good enough. This looks like being a long time yet.
General Sir John Hackett, Lees Knowles Lectures,
Cambridge, 1962

IN THE SIX YEAR gap between leaving *Duke of York* and journeying to Capetown to join my first and only post-war sea appointment, *HMS Bermuda*, I had managed to infuriate one engineer-in-chief as a result of my two reports from the Pacific; been provisionally appointed to the Admiralty naval staff and as a result of his anger dis-appointed; sent into limbo to talk round the schools for the new electrical branch; be rescued by the new and first Fisher-trained engineer-in-chief; be sent to Birmingham University to study petroleum technology and finally to join his intellectual élite (dagger) officers at Bath as inspector in charge of the fuels and lubricants section. I had also married Pam Berthon, the daughter of my mentor at Keyham and my chief in *Hood*; and we had produced two daughters.

Within 24 hours of our arrival in Capetown we had all contracted Apricot Tummy, the local equivalent of Malta Dog. The next day I was well enough to join my ship whereupon we sailed for exercises in Saldanha Bay, a little way up the coast, leaving my wife to house hunt. By the time we had returned, a week later, she had found a small bungalow we could just afford on our £72 monthly budget. She had done magnificently: our new home had a marvellous view and was within 15 minutes walk of the ship, for as yet we had no car.

My predecessor had been in charge of the wardroom wines

• *The bungalow Pam found*

and spirits and, wisely, had filled a number of double bottoms with varying liquors to help show the flag, giving hospitality, at our own expense, with an occasional subvention from the commander-in-chief's hospitality fund. As our parish stretched from Lourenco Marques to Dakar and back via St Helena and Ascension, and all ports between, this task was formidable and expensive. A typical Capetown party was, for me, the first of many since the organisation of our floating public house now devolved on my shoulders. Of somewhat greater importance, this was the first time I had been in charge of an engineering department on my own other than for a few days. On our first trip to Saldanha Bay I was necessarily a spectator. The senior engineer, with a jaw like a prize fighter, was clearly not to be gainsaid even if I had contemplated any immediate changes.

As I have so often found it is the small details that have unexpected impacts: in this case it was hot water. After leaving Simonstown I was met by the surgeon-commander, a normally polite and charming physician. *No bloody hot water again,* he complained bitterly. Chatting to the captain that evening on the bridge he rather hesitantly pointed out that the hot water tap in his sea cabin was always dry. It was a design error he had been told. Was it? I promised to investigate. My department's response was entirely negative, little of Fisher's *community of sentiment* seeming to exist amongst the (E) officers. My experience with Berthon in the *Hood* struck me forcibly: check and check again and start with the ship's drawings. I have often criticised the Royal Corps of Naval Constructors but I never believed them fools. Of course there was a hot water pump. In the past it had been enclosed and hidden behind a well-secured Royal Marines great-coat locker. For many years, out of sight and now paint encrusted, it had rested virginal and untouched.

My next battle was less easy. To reduce accumulations of soot between the boiler tubes, ships of *Bermuda's* vintage had been fitted with steam blowers to vent the detritus up the funnel. Worked once or twice a day the blowers greatly reduced the incidence of soot removal by hand. But what goes up must come down and showing the flag meant that *Bermuda* at all times had to appear spotless, so use of the soot-blowers had been forbidden. By putting the ship off course, so that the wind was abeam, it soon became an acceptable twice-daily routine again. But at first I had to appear on the bridge myself to show that the operation could be performed without desecration.

These two minor incidents indicated that the entente between executive officers and engineers, always envisaged by Fisher and firmly cemented in wartime, was falling apart in peacetime. There were faults on both sides; on mine I had to try to remedy them. I had also been appointed fleet engineer officer responsible for the mobility of several frigates on the station which post gave me an interesting access as unofficial engineering adviser to the newly-formed South African Navy, many of whose officers and ratings had fought so valiantly to keep Tobruk supplied. And it meant that I was on the staff of our remarkable Commander-in-Chief, Admiral Sir Herbert (Bertie) Packer.

Although my wife and I had now been married five years, we had never attended a full dress naval dinner party together. So it was with some trepidation that, fully rigged, we embarked in our recently acquired and very second-hand Morris 8 for Admiralty House. Guests included the Springbok rugger side, triumphantly back from a tour of the UK. After dinner the commander-in-chief and some cronies disappeared to play bridge leaving Lady Packer to preside in the drawing room. The hospitality had already been plentiful and powerful, as was the subsequent Cape brandy. Lady Packer came from a well-known Afrikaaner family and shared in the triumphs of the rugger side. She was as ready with her ukelele as the Springboks were ready with their songs. Most rugger choruses are known to (E) officers and my Keyham memories soon returned and our hostess seemed to enjoy it as much as the Springboks. Much of my time however was spent speculating

• *The author, left, receives the OBE found in the secretary's bottom drawer*

whether my Pam's eyes would return to their sockets. Life in the Wrens, she assured me, had never been like this.

It was midsummer when I received two identical cables from England, one from my in-laws and one from my brother. Each congratulated me, though we had no idea for what. In the hopes that our names might have come up in one of the sweepstakes Pam and I were apt to go in for, she wired her mother for more details. To this came a financially disappointing answer: the OBE. As we had heard nothing officially and the newspapers took 14 days to reach South Africa, we kept mum.

In due course two small pieces of ribbon arrived to be sewn on to my uniforms; but there was no explanation as to why the Admiralty signal with the birthday awards had not been repeated to the c-in-c. The letter accompanying the ribbon explained that the award came for helping to straighten out the navy's oil affairs and I assumed that when we returned to the UK I would attend an investiture. It was a surprise, some six months later, to be rung up by the secretary to the new Commander-in-Chief, Admiral Sir Peveril William-Powlett (*Fiji's* captain when she was sunk coming to the rescue of *Naiad* in the battle for Crete) asking if I had ever received my decoration.

I've found one in the bottom drawer of my predecessor's desk, it must be your's, he went on.

One blazing hot Sunday off Luanda, to the fury of the whole sweating ship's company, the commander-in-chief ordered full ceremonial divisons. Watched by a markedly sullen audience, the missing order was presented to me without the presence, sadly, of the only person who, by her ability to keep the home fires burning, usually without my help, had made this recognition possible.

Showing the flag involved entertaining variously coloured inhabitants of Africa from Portuguese East Africa (now Mozambique) to Dakar, several thousand miles to the north-west. In Angola's capital, Luanda, another commander and I challenged the black permanent secretaries of Angola's Housing and Education to a round of golf. With a temperature of more than 100 °F in the shade, 12 huge caddies accompanied us: four bounding ahead to preserve our golf balls from birds and animals; four carrying our clubs effortlessly and a further four bearing on thir heads ice, glasses, whisky and bottles of soda with which we were revived at each hole. By the time we reached the next green nature had ensured that re-fuelling was necessary. Despite these unusual conditions we won, thanks largely to Commander Humphry-Salwey who, with a scratch handicap, achieved a psychological superiority by casually throwing down his wrapped golf ball and, equally casually, hitting it with a spectacular explosion of the paper wrapping further down the course than the rest of us. He drank less whisky than I did, and I drank much less than our kindly, cultured and knowledgeable opponents. On this remarkably high note I ended my golfing career.

The Gold Coast or Ghana as we must call it, then no longer provided the thrills of landing through the surf. But the hospitality of the Gold Coast regiment at Takoradi was warm and friendly. However, later in the evening when I overheard two immense Sandhurst-trained Gold Coast regiment (Ghanaian) officers discussing how long it would take to seize the commander-in-chief, remove his shoes and socks, up-end him, blacken the soles of his feet and leave his footmarks on the ceiling, we thought it wise to tell Admiral Sir Peveril William-Powlett that it was time to leave.

As the first British warship for many years to visit the Spanish colony of Fernando Po we were welcomed ecstatically. In the wardroom draw for the multiplicity of invitations showered on us, I drew a visit to the spotless maternity hospital where a Spanish-trained black gynaecologist skilfully delivered a couple of babies for my particular edification. At Lagos we nearly disrupted Nigeria's move into the Commonwealth. The admiral's barge and captain's motor boat, crammed with paramount chiefs, their ample wives and their Umbrella Men, suffered from water-contaminated fuel and drifted past the ship on a steady 12-knot current apparently bound for America. Had the ship's launch, luckily alongside at the time, been similarly effected

Bermuda would have had to raise steam in a hurry and try to catch them before they disappeared over the horizon. It was treated as a great joke and the chiefs and their consorts so enjoyed their refreshments that some plates of sandwiches and a few bottles disappeared into capacious handbags. The Umbrella Men were not so lucky. They were not permitted to eat , drink or even furl their umbrellas under our best awning. The resultant holes made a great deal of work for the usually less than fully occupied sailmaker who was the only one not to see the joke.

Dakar, *jolie Dakar* to anyone who has read *Beau Geste,* was a joy. The dinner in the governor's residence with Spahi officers and Arabs in their differing uniforms and burnous, all speaking faultless French and apparently anxious to forget and forgive the Royal Navy's attack on the city a decade or so before, was one of the most civilised functions I have ever attended.

Cable and Wireless employees in Ascension were particularly hospitable to those who braved the heavy swell and the hand-worked crane with a basket on the end into which we leapt as the boat rose on the waves. To the Royal Marines, Ascension is special. The garrison, sent there when Napoleon was banished by us to St Helena, was maintained pointlessly for years after his death. On the top of the island there is a cap of lush grass where cows graze. Near the landing stage there is a little church wherein there is a memorial to a Royal Marine *who died while driving the daily cart.* In 1952 the jeep, bringing fresh milk from the farm down to the settlement, was still called *The daily cart.* St Helena, too, was an interesting interlude. Napoleon now lies in Les Invalides but the governor's ancient tortoise, still surviving, had been alive during the emperor's incarceration. The children and teenagers who met us wearing naval caps were not, as we first thought, an embryo Sea Cadet Corps. The cap ribbons, all of which emanated from ships at one time or another on the South Atlantic Station, served only to indicate paternity.

After the autumn cruise Pam, now pregnant, was looking forward to having our third child in South Africa. Nevertheless she helped me greatly in a tricky remit from the captain 'to take an interest in the midshipmen'. Both he and the commander-in-chief had been disappointed at the midshipmen's poor perform-ance in the ship's regatta so I was asked to choose and then coach their gig's crew. The commander was agreeable but the Snottie's Nurse, the executive officer in charge of the midshipmen, was less happy so I had to be circumspect. The intense heat of the West African cruise (we had no air conditioning) and the interminable - compulsory - parties and dances they attended, had dampened the normal gunroom fire. By devious cosseting including stupendous brunches, large late lazy breakfasts on sundays and picnics with our children, Pam did much to restore them to their effervescent norm. They were a delightful lot anyway and responded enthusiastically to my training in the gig by sweeping the board in the combined Royal and South African Navy's regatta.

Murphy, that mythical being who manages to upset the best-laid plans of engineers, had not had many opportunities to assault me since the *Duke of York*, apart from the water in the fuel incident in Lagos but now he determined to make redress. The c-in-c decided to mount a combined exercise with the South African navy whom we had taught to fuel at sea, or thought we had. At my request that evolution was included at the end of a day which included gunnery and torpedo firings. Most of the South African cabinet were to be on board *Bermuda* together with a posse of the Capetown press. All went well: the guns fired and mock torpedo attacks by the SAN were a triumph with not even a near collision. After an extremely good lunch the cabinet and the commander-in-chief assembled on the lower bridge as a South African destroyer approached gingerly. The hoses went over and were connected in record time and pumping started but after only a few minutes the destroyer petty officer mistakenly shut off the inlet to one tank before opening up another. The hose split and started waving in the air whereupon *Bermuda's* upper deck, and all those on it including the cabinet, were doused in heavy fuel oil. As the *Cape Times* headlined succinctly, with an accompanying photograph, *Bermuda strikes it rich.*

• *Bermuda gets well oiled. Helping to clear up the mess*

On our return to Simonstown tragic news awaited us: *Bermuda* was to return home, recommission and then join the Mediterranean fleet. Pam, with a baby now well on the way, would have to return to UK alone - two children and a mother's help apart - through the tropics and from one hot summer to, as it turned out, a bitter spring. Happily we got her a passage in the same steamer as some more mobile wives and, apart from a spectacular faint whilst passing through customs at Southampton, all was well.

After the fuelling debacle the commander-in-chief had been rather cool. My reputation suffered further following the wardroom's farewell dance, the arrangements for which fell into my lap. Admiral and Lady William-Powlett had an attractive daughter who was as anxious to come to the dance as the gunroom was to welcome her. Admiral and wife were less keen, so Pam and I undertook to keep an eye on her while the commander-in-chief and Lady William-Powlett looked after their official guests. Although I did not see her leave, I assumed his daughter had been taken home by car. Next day the commander-in-chief was even cooler when he revealed that after a worried night for him and his wife, his daughter was restored to Admiralty House on the back of a midshipman's loudly revving motor-bike in the early hours of the morning. Thirty years later I attended a seminar on *The church and the bomb*. An intelligent curate taking part turned out to be Admiral William-Powlett's grandson, then at Holy Trinity Brompton: he was delighted to learn of one of his mother's early escapades.

On arrival in Devonport a new ship's company - and my relief - came on board. I was to accompany the ship to Gibraltar whence I would fly home, but Murphy had another trick up his sleeve. I was returning from the yard offices when the dockyard fire brigade came clanging up behind. Learning that the fire was in *Bermuda* I hopped onto the first engine and arrived at the ship at the same time as the gunner, the only other officer remaining from the previous commission. The new ship's company on the quarterdeck was being addressed by the new captain when dense black smoke was spotted coming from Y turret; even the newest young sailor straight from a training establishment was aware that turrets sit on top of magazines which can explode. Someone had been sent to fetch the magazine flooding keys but in the speed of recommissioning, the new team had not yet been shown where the magazine flooding valves were.   A few understandably timorous souls were already gazing longingly over the sides into the muddy waters of the Hamoaze.   Donning smoke helmets the gunner and I crept into the turret where, under his guidance, we soon found the trouble.   Batteries had been put on charge by the previous commission - and forgotten.   As this was my last ship, Murphy gave up the ghost - at least for a while.   The Admiralty, whither I was bound, would be perhaps less easy to penetrate!

So it was once more 'from sea to shore'.   And, though I did not know it then, for the last time.   Again my reports from the Pacific caught up with me.   I was appointed to the office of the extra naval assistant to the second sea lord for engineering personnel, known as EAP, a rear-admiral (E).   To him I found I was to be responsible for the appointment of all engineering officers from commander (E) downwards.   And, as it turned out, also as an assessor on Vice Admiral Sir Aubrey Mansergh's committee which hoped to re-inject the Fisher concept of one General List of officers, which I had so strongly advocated, into the post-world war two naval officer corps.   From there I was sent as second-in-command to Manadon with a directive so to change the routines.   And then back to the Admiralty again first, on promotion to captain, as secretary to Lord Murray's committee examining the academic entry arrangements for officers, then as assistant engineer-in-chief (personnel) and, finally, as naval assistant to the third sea lord and controller of the navy.   A ten-year stint of quite hard work after leaving *Bermuda.*

In Austria in 1934 I had been on the fringes of international events when Dr Dollfuss was murdered.   I had been arrested by Italian troops when climbing on the Austro-Italian border and plied with chianti while my papers were examined.   I had seen the swastikas in fire lit on the mountain side by Hitler's adherents and met and drunk beer with Schuschnigg's *Heimwehr.*   Later, in that summer of the great Nuremberg Rally, I had sat round camp fires with the *wandervogel* and listened with some approbation to their haunting melodies.   It all seemed so much better than the squalor and filth of Tyneside to which Reggie Churchill, our chaplain at Keyham, had taken us.   Germany appeared an attractive alternative or so, naively, I came to believe.   The villages and towns were spotless, the beer was good, the lodgings cheap, the 'natives' happy and apparently friendly.   Later still, in the *Hood* in Gibraltar, we had all become good friends with the *Deutchland.*   Then came the war. And in the aftermath, in my time in the fuels and lubricants section, I had worked for the Brussels Treaty organisation and for NATO in its early days and had seen a western europe desperately afraid that Russia would march.

Masaryk murdered, the Berlin blockade, the Korean war, developments in Indo-China, Kenya and Cyprus, the rape of Hungary, the post war fate of Poland and Czechoslovakia, the advent of thermonuclear weapons, all contributed to my realisation that our sunset dreams of September 2, 1945 in Tokyo Bay were mirages. I was glad to be appointed to the Imperial Defence College to learn about all this and to discuss where the navy should be going.

One day in St James' Park I met, not for the first time, Mr (now the late Sir William) Cook, a great scientist and then head of the Royal Naval Scientific Service and a staunch exponent of the need to improve the navy's mobility. He told me some of the repercussions of the new H-bomb, its effect on the course of warfare and mankind. We stood on the then new bridge watching the ducks while he rehearsed his fears as to the difficulties of making military men and politicians, in every country, appreciate the problem of control. I mentioned Hiroshima and Nagasaki whose bombs he likened to a hand grenade compared with a 2000lb block buster. That, he felt, was the danger: people would feel that the damage, while terrible, was containable. In fact, he said, mankind could now effectively destroy itself. I realised at that moment how much I had to learn.

Earlier I had applied for a staff course and been denied it as 'too young and too junior'. Two years later I was told I was 'too old and too senior'. So early in the fifties I joined the Royal United Services Institute and have been a member ever since. In the *Naval Review*, a privately circulated journal, I found a receptive vehicle for acquainting the Admiralty with my views on current naval problems. In the *RUSI Journal* I broadcast these views more widely. The supine attitude of the many admirals in the audience when Field Marshal Montgomery delivered his 1954 RUSI lecture, *A look through a window at world war three* and the facile way he and Lord Tedder wrote off the navy riled. Montgomery's targets were large aircraft carriers, with which I agreed, but he also implied that only a minimal navy was needed to convoy merchant ships into ports, for which small surface ships and submarines only were necessary. Sea control, he said, would be exercised by land-based airpower with freight carried by short take off and landing (STOL) jumbo aircraft rather than merchant ships. Clearly he failed to appreciate the logistic problems, the supply of fuel particularly, that his thesis postulated. I differed too from his view that NATO planning should be based on the use of airborne nuclear and thermonuclear weapons which was precisely the pit into which, as Sir William Cook had forecast, military men would fall. I received a polite reply from the field marshal's aide-de-camp. Though I claim no responsibility for Montgomery's change of attitude over the next few years, in fact he later advocated the need for seapower to be exercised over, on and under the surface of the world's oceans.

This little foray spurred me on and over the next few years the RUSI published *The one open highway, World population and British strategy, The Royal Navy's role in the defence service of the eighties, The mobility of the fleet, All oceans lead to England,* and *Peace is our profession.* In the last of these I propounded my Constabulary Concept of roving nuclear-propelled naval task forces prepared for any peacetime disaster or military eventuality, an idea still bandied about. Sadly the Royal Navy, hedged in by economic restraints and unimaginative politicians, has never subscribed to nuclear surface propulsion which would remove it from the tyranny of overseas oil supplies. British naval reaction to these articles was ever disappointing; Admirals Mountbatten and Le Fanu only offering any encouragement. Strangely, I thought then, army officers responded enthusiastically. I have heard since that my articles were compulsory reading at the Army Staff College. More encouraging still were the letters from the US navy. Indeed one commander came to Bath to cross-question me. However I attribute Admiral Crowe's later appointment as chairman of the US joint chiefs of staff to his remarkable wisdom and vision rather than mine! The USN deputy chief of naval operations, Admiral Benson, wrote deprecating my view that the UK should not build big carriers and for asserting, as I had, that 'air power projection over land' was an improper role for a navy. Best of all Admiral Thursfield, then editor of *Brasseys Armed Forces Year Book,* commissioned me to write a chapter on *Sea power* in the 1963 edition which gave me an opportunity to excoriate the British chiefs of staff for their blinkered concentration on the threat to the central front in Europe to the neglect of the flanks and other non-nuclear Soviet options for exerting pressure on the west. The same article involved me in disputation at the Imperial Defence College to which I was appointed in 1963. Best of all it brought about a lasting friendship, until his early death, with Air Commodore Neil Cameron, later Marshal of the Royal Air Force Lord Cameron of Balhousie, KT, GCB, CBE, DSO, DFC, our most brilliant course student. Early in our time at the Imperial Defence College Professor Alastair Buchan, then director of the International Institute for Strategic Studies, wrote an article in *The Times* calling for strategic studies in our universities. By implication there was criticism of the services and Whitehall for their lack of original thought with which several of us agreed. I cannot recall how Cameron, Brigadier Kenneth Hunt and I came together to endorse his remarks in *The Times*. However we drafted a letter urging that the service policy staffs should participate in Professor Buchan's ideas. We went on to suggest that the RUSI would provide the ideal centre where academics, industry, the services, Whitehall and Westminster could debate strategic issues within a practical economic framework. Air Chief Marshal Sir Hugh Constantine, the commandant and a friend to us all, quickly consented to our letter's publication and we took it by hand to *The Times* on monday morning. By thursday it had not appeared so we gave up hope. As we were going in to the afternoon lecture, I was called to the phone to find Admiral Sir Ronald Brockman, for so many years secretary to Lord Mountbatten (then chief of the defence staff) on the other end. Furiously he demanded to know what the three of us thought we were doing writing publicly, and summoned me to Storey's Gate. By now the others were in the lecture so I took off alone to Brockman's office.

CDS is very angry. You must know serving officers cannot write to the papers, I was told.

When I replied that we had the commandant's permission Brockman broke into a grin. *I know,* he said, *but he should not have given it to you. Anyway the editor of* The Times *sent the letter here and CDS is adamant that it should not be published. However he fully agrees with all you say and has circulated your letter to the chiefs of staff for some sort of action. He also says you should get it published in the RUSI Journal.*

With that we had to be content.

It has taken 25 years under a succession of enthusiastic chairmen and a long line of able directors and secretaries, including the late Air Vice-Marshal Paddy Menaul, CB, CBE, DFC, AFC,

RAF (retd) and the present incumbent, Group Captain Bolton RAF (retd) to accomplish most, if not even more, than we recommended. With some honourable exceptions, few politicians take the time or trouble to comprehend the life and death issues which a prolonged peace tends to obscure and which, often, the media so grossly misrepresent. The year-long Imperial Defence College course gave us a chance to think, to talk to other students and dispute with the lecturers. Above all it brought friendships to oil Whitehall's wheels in the years to come. It also made us conscious of the problems of other countries, whose students were represented at Seaford House.

The three of us who wrote the original letter, with a few others who could make the time available, felt that there was more we could do. As the commandant, Michael (later Sir Michael) Stewart from the Foreign and Commonwealth office and the three senior directing staff concurred, about a dozen of us arranged a series of buffet suppers and additional lecturers of our own choosing from a wide field of non-service activities.

Towards the end of our time, and with the active help of Mr, later The Rt Hon Sir Michael Palliser, GCMG, permanent secretary at the Foreign and Commonwealth Office, we formed a small dining club, vowing to meet frequently as we did for nearly 17 years. Prime ministers and ex prime ministers, foreign secretaries and secretaries of state for defence and others holding high political office, civil servants, senior police officers, famous industrialists and trade unionists, have all accepted invitations to expound their views. Only the Soviet threat now seems constant and sometimes more, sometimes less, imminent. By the eighties most of the original group had retired. Some had died and all were getting long in the tooth and finding the journey to London increasingly difficult and expensive so we turned to the 1968 course to join us. In their enthusiasm they swamped us. The 63/ 68 club is far larger but, sadly, a less cosy group which meets occasionally if with less regularity. Our 1963 course colleague who reached furthest up the greasy pole was John Ironsi, a Nigerian of vast bulk, omnivorous sexual appetite and one of the kindest, though perhaps not the cleverest, of men. We were saddened when as his country's president, we learned of his assassination.

As part of a group I visited North Africa, Malaysia, Singapore, Australia and New Zealand but the most depressing visit was to the British Army of the Rhine. There was nothing wrong with the enthusiasm, morale and fighting efficiency of our soldiers. What depressed us were the scenarios displayed, all envisaging the immediate use of tactical nuclear weapons which, inevitably, we felt must lead to all-out nuclear war. I understand now, as I did then, the original political imperatives that required British forces to be in Germany till 1998 or longer. But I have always believed, and I found others did too, that the main purpose of the Soviet forces was and is to intimidate western Europe and thus make subversion more effective. The UK is not only the linchpin of NATO but also its jugular vein. By concentrating the bulk of our army and air forces in Germany, as the Brussels treaty so expensively insists, we not only reduce funds available for the navy, thus inviting outright blackmail by blockade (or 'quarantine' as Kennedy wisely called it in the 1962 Cuban blockade) but we leave our country open to overhead assault. The Soviet Spetznaz (SAS type) brigades, now Afghanistan war-conditioned, and the eight Soviet airborne divisions can drop by night and seize the swathe of Anglo-US airfields from Norfolk to Gloucestershire. NATO would be emasculated. Thus the scenarios displayed to us, envisaging only a Soviet thrust by their Shock Armies across the German plain and NATO's immediate use of tactical nuclear weapons, appeared altogether too narrow and unimaginative a concept of the threat, even 25 years ago.

Theoretically the passage of years means nothing to the Kremlin in its pursuit of world hegemony. But time is no longer on the Soviet side as we then imagined it was: the buds of freedom are blossoming behind the Iron Curtain. The law of colonial ingratitude has started to operate in the different ethnic republics as it has against all recent empires. For good USSR reasons, Gorbachev is pursuing a different strategy from his predecessors' more simplistic one of brute force.

Germany was born out of war into a nation state only in 1871. Yet in the following 60 years she provoked two world wars. The German state has had no individual alliances with the west. Gorbachev no doubt recalls the Bismarckian doctrine, *That whenever good relations existed between Germany and Russia both countries flourished. But whenever the links between them weakened, both countries suffered.* So a united Germany is his ultimate target in some sort of mutual arms-limiting, industry-boosting agreement with the Kremlin, coupled with the withdrawal of British and

American troops. General de Gaulle wrote in his war memoirs, *France is true to herself only when she stands in the front rank: only great enterprises can neutralize the poison of disunity her people carry in their veins.* Mitterand understands this well so France will not permit Germany to leave her behind while engaging in some sort of entente with the Soviets. I believe that Soviet Russia as an ally, in the sort of Europe de Gaulle described *as from the Atlantic to the Urals,* is still part of an entirely cynical French foreign policy. NATO's policies must change radically or wither in the next decade.

Violence begets violence so if Gorbachev's long term plans for economic rehabilitation fail and civil war or major unrest in the Soviet Union occurs, the world will be imperilled.

Historically 1963 was towards the end of the old traditional Imperial Defence College course. Today life in the College is probably more organised and certainly more serious, because few, if any, of the students have ever tasted the disorganisation of war. Certainly none has seen the heartbreak, muddle, beastliness, chaos and stupidity of a prolonged conflict as our generation did. Conscientiously they prepare to excel us in the management of violence . . . and good luck to them. If the chiefs of staff are now looking at a wider, more complex picture then to the Royal College of Defence Studies and the Royal United Service Institute for Defence Studies must go much of the credit.

• *The star of the show after his trip in a non-operatic Phantom*

CHAPTER 14

British Naval Attaché, Washington DC, April 1967-September 1969

Always remember that you are the trustee for the Royal Navy in North America
Admiral Hyman G Rickover USN, June 1967

NO ATTACHÉ CAN OPERATE effectively without a willing, hardworking wife. Happily for me, Pam, nurtured in a naval family, a wartime petty officer in the WRNS and with 16 moves under her belt in 20 years of married life, appeared outwardly to have few qualms. Indeed she was allegedly looking forward to sharing my load for which neither of us had any training. Before we had even left our home near Chippenham the Board of Admiralty's flag lieutenant rang to enquire when he should say farewell on their behalf after we had boarded the *RMS Queen Elizabeth.* My reply that such a courtesy was unnecessary prompted the suggestion that someone should supervise the conveyance into the hold of our baggage for a two-year stint in Washington, which was how we met again Mrs Hicks, of the department of sea transport. She had performed miracles when sending us to South Africa years earlier, had dealt with the paper work of getting us to the States and now accompanied by six strong sailors she met us with our 32 bags, suitcases, trunks and packing cases at Southampton station.

As a civil servant Mrs Hicks had attended no leadership courses or given words of command on the Gunnery School parade ground: either would have been quite superrogatory. In no time our luggage was stowed in a truck and we were quayside-bound by limousine. Once installed in the two cabins, my wife and I and two of our three teenage daughters awaited a few relatives to see us off. *Have you arranged suitable refreshments?* demanded Mrs Hicks. Worried as we were about money we had done no such thing. *You don't have to pay,* she replied rightly interpreting my hesitation and took off like a missile. A procession of stewards, bearing bottles and trays of delicacies undreamt of in the Le Bailly family, appeared simultaneously with our guests. Thanks to our stalwart OC Troops, we were ready for them.

Not wishing to accompany us to the States, our guests duly left when a broadcast so instructed. Mrs Hicks, her Robin Hood hat now askew and clearly worried at my lack of grip, appeared to contemplate coming with us or, at least, disembarking down the jacob's ladder with the pilot. With seconds to spare we managed to escort her to the gangway, held only by the crane, where a desperate petty officer steered her into his limousine. Dear Mrs Hicks, we shall none of us forget her or what she did for us on that nerve-wracking day. When the voyage ended, which had its hilarious moments thanks in part to Peter Sellers with whom we became friendly, we sadly missed Mrs Hicks. As I had driven the family on deck to see the Manhattan windows flashing in the sunrise, we felt pretty sleepy by the time we were ashore, so the words of Rear-Admiral Peter Compston, my experienced predecessor and his wife, fell on somewhat unreceptive ears. Next day, after a long, dirty, foodless train journey, we reached Washington DC in uncertain tempers and embarked in a pompous Daimler driven by a cheerful Royal Marine corporal. Rain was belting down, a windscreen wiper fell off as we left the station followed later in Massachusetts Avenue by part of the exhaust pipe before we reached 4807 Newport Avenue, our new home.

Our first crisis was inability to dismiss the accomplished but expensive cook we had inherited. Asserting quite wrongly that she had security of tenure, Emelia simply would not go. However, invited shortly after we arrived to the new minister's house, my wife Pam heard that their cook had left unexpectedly. Quick as a flash a willing Emelia was translated to where her talents were fully appreciated and better rewarded. We would have to conjure up a replacement cook when needed but here again Pam's magic prevailed: Katie Snow was a lady of uncertain ethnic origin with superlative culinary expertise. Occasionally as when, with an eldritch shriek of happy laughter, she emerged from the kitchen bearing a christmas pudding dripping burning brandy, slightly singeing in passing the bouffant hair style of the Dean of Washington's wife, she had to be restrained. But never was she defeated.

Nathaniel Campbell, a tall negro, straight from *Gone with the wind* and indeed from Alabama, with a vast laugh and an unquenchable sense of humour, attended to our cocktail parties, accompanied by up to half a dozen equally deft and willing helpers. The apotheosis of our two visiting teams, Katie and Nathaniel and his tribe of assistants, occurred later at our middle daughter's wedding. Their humour, skill and general willingness so impressed the new ambassador and his wife, that they were all taken on temporarily at the British embassy until a new permanent staff could be recruited. Even from this olympian height they all turned up to help with our farewell parties.

Throughout there was need to stay solvent: no one had told us that if you overdraw at your Stateside bank all credit facilities are removed and credit cards invalidated. Thanks to Emelia's penchant for the most expensive foods we were down to three dollars at the end of our first month when the next pay cheque just saved us. Pam, like the other attachés' wives had to account item by item for our guests, 1184 in our first year, who ate and drank in our house.

Initially the socially dominant figure in our world was an English lady with American citizenship. Widowed in the war she had been one of Eisenhower's staff in Europe. After surviving a major air crash she became personal assistant to the head of the British navy staff. Now remarried she had seen admirals come and go. Unfortunately her thirteenth admiral had neither the inclination nor the resources to aspire to the grandeur that this patriotic lady deemed proper, but after a few sticky patches Mrs Phillips (Maggie to most of Washington) adjusted to our views and served us patiently and loyally.

Pam's greatest triumph was as chairman of the British element of the YWCA international fair at a great Washington hotel. Had some of the British shops and stores, whose goods she wheedled from them and displayed and sold, followed up with similar verve our balance of payments would have improved noticeably. But the lunch party, several months after our arrival, which she cooked from scratch at four hours' notice, ran it pretty close. Her good food, impeccably served by our faithful Royal

Marine driver, Corporal Sims, prompted 10 congressmen, including two chairmen of the Senate and House Armed Services Committee to congratulate me on the first class cook provided by the Admiralty. More important to Britain they left our house a little comforted that, in abandoning our role east of Suez, we would still be at their side in the Atlantic.

We were lucky that we already knew the head of the British Joint Services Mission, Admiral Sir Nigel Henderson and his wife Catharine. She had launched the new *Naiad* from Yarrow's Yard when we had all stayed at *Cloak*, Sir Eric Yarrow's home. She was the first to call and offer help. The departing minister, Sir Michael Stewart, whom I had known at the Imperial Defence College, took me round the chancery desks on my first morning. Thereafter I felt at home with the able and always welcoming diplomats, many to become ambassadors in the years ahead. Initially Pam and I stood in awe of the ambassador, Sir Patrick Dean and his wife Patricia. But they were both enormously kind and when they discovered that Pam, a keen gardener, was horrified at the apology for a garden at 4807, shrubs and roses and a few small trees, with some strong men to help her plant them, miraculously appeared. Curiously the embassy butler, Charlie Dean, who might well have stepped out of *Upstairs, Downstairs* had lived in the next village to my Gloucestershire home. As a child he had received kindness from my mother and so constituted himself our ally. The military attaché, Major-General (later Sir) Richard Fyfe, a famously brave officer, had served in Malta before the war and we had been acquainted. He and his wife, like Air Vice Marshal Franks, the air attaché and his wife, made us welcome.

After buying a seemingly enormous, but by American standards modest, Ford Fairlane for £1000, passing our driving test, over fed at great cost by Emelia, guided by Maggie Phillips, one daughter seeking a job and the other in a local school, we were ready to assault Washington. Matters got off to a rousing start: the Egyptians suddenly blockaded the Straits of Tirah thus cutting off Israel's access to the Red Sea and Indian Ocean. The UN secretary-general unexpectedly withdrew the UNO peacekeeping force in the Sinai desert: suddenly Israel and Egypt/Jordan were at war. The prime minister, Harold Wilson, contemplated flying over to see President Johnson signalling that he would rely for naval advice on the attaché. This rather set the cat amongst the staff pigeons unused to having an (E) specialist in command. But

I was fortunate. Admiral Sir Nigel Henderson, immensely experienced and with infinite tact, let me know he would always be available for advice should I so wish. In fact the prime minister never came. There was a proposal that a UN naval task force should sail into the Gulf of Aqaba and the Australian and Netherlands navies signalled they would join the RN and USN in this enterprise. So Rear Admiral Bartosik, a British naval officer with the sort of fighting instinct and record one would expect from his Polish background, flew over to consult with the USN and the State Department, the denizens of Washington's aptly named Foggy Bottom. His forthright, clearcut proposals scared the latter stiff but Sir Michael Stewart, our minister, calmed them and international diplomacy stopped the fighting, leaving Israel in occupation of Sinai, including the Egyptian oilfields and the entrance to the Gulf of Aqaba. It was an interesting baptism for a new attaché and it helped me to get to know the head of chancery (later Sir John Killick, an outstanding ambassador to Moscow) and Alan Urwick, son of Mr Urwick the famous management consultant with whom I had worked in Bath) and now Sir Alan Urwick, former ambassador in Egypt and Black Rod (designate).

In our 30-month stint in Washington DC we weathered

• The 1967 Arab/Israeli war

• Two major UK defence reviews, the first intimating (to the Pentagon) that British withdrawal from the Far East did not mean withdrawal from the Indian Ocean/Persian Gulf area; and the second saying that it did

• Devaluation of sterling with consequential difficulties for all expatriates

• A dozen visits by naval commanders in chief, naval members of the Board of Admiralty and various ministers in the defence field

• Two visits by AF Lord Mountbatten and one by AF Sir Caspar John

• Six successful Polaris test firings from Cape Canaveral

• Start to finish of the Phantom aircraft procurement programme

• Visits by 55 HM ships to US ports

• Supervision of a transatlantic air race

THE *Bellevue Stratford*

Broad and Walnut Streets
Philadelphia, Pa. 19102

CABLE ADDRESS
BELLSTRAT

TELETYPE 215 569-9703
PEnnypacker 5-0700
AREA CODE 215

13th March 1968

My dear Lois,

      I am writing to thank you very much indeed
for the enormous amount of personal trouble which
you took to organise my week-end visit with Ronnie
Brockman to Washington.

      I fully realise how difficult it must have
been to fit in the various luncheons and dinners
which my friends wanted to give, as well as the
rest of the programme, and the result from my
point of view was excellent.

      In particular the talks with Rickover and
Tom Moorer which you organised were of great
value to me and I hope my letter to Sir Solly
Zuckerman may prove of help to what you are trying
to put over.

      I heard on all hands what a very high opinion
the Americans have formed of you and I find this
particularly gratifying as it was I, when First Sea
Lord, who established the principle that Flag
Officers from the non-seaman branches would make
excellent candidates for some of the jobs previously
the preserve of seamen. Your own success is a
great vindication for this principle.

      Once more all my thanks.

Yours very sincerely

Mountbatten of Burma

- Change of president and hence of the whole administration

- The relief of Admiral Thomas Moorer USN as supreme allied commander, Atlantic, by Admiral Ephraim Holmes USN

- The relief of Admiral McDonald USN as chief of naval operations by Admiral Moorer. Four secretaries of the navy and changes in the appointment of nearly every senior US naval officer afloat and ashore

- The hi-jacking of the *USS Pueblo* by North Korea

- Loss of a US hunter-killer nuclear submarine off the Azores

- A change of British ambassador, minister, head of chancery and most desk officers in the British embassy

- A change in the head of the British joint services mission

- The assassinations of Martin Luther King and Robert Kennedy

- The trek of the negroes from the deep south and the establishment of 'Resurrection City' in Washington's fairest park

- Robert Kennedy's funeral

- Riots involving the burning and looting of the centre of Washington and the injection of 12,000 troops and a number of tanks and armoured vehicles to enforce a curfew

- The campus revolt

- The attempt to storm the Pentagon by 100,000 anti-Vietnam protesters

- Arrest of the British cruise liner *SS Carmania* by the US Coast Guard, for lack of proper fire precaution arrangements, when full of passengers

- Visits by six major UK committees all involving the British navy staff

- A comprehensive tour of US shipbuilding facilities and an investigation into the feasibility of modular construction for war and merchant ships

- Britain's invasion of Anguilla

- The death and state funeral of President Eisenhower

- Celebrations to mark NATO's twentieth anniversary

- Complex negotiations on the law of the sea bed

- Supervision of UK defence sales until their volume required a separate organisation

- Chairmanship of the military staff committee to the UN security council during the controversial election of a new international secretary

- Establishment of the Standing Naval Force, Atlantic (STANAVFOR-LANT)

- Visits by *HMS Fife* and *Glamorgan* to Washington

- The journey to the moon.

These were only the major events. In the background was always the interminable Vietnam war in which Britain played no part. Our task was made no easier as we came to meet service people, the bodies of whose sons and brothers were being brought home for burial in the enlarged Arlington national cemetery. We tried to help by meeting the giant Starlifters as they brought the wounded to Andrewes Air Force base where our wives did what they could to comfort the whey-faced young men lacking limbs lost in that bloody booby-trap war.

I had a namesake in Washington, possibly a remote cousin. General Ben Le Bailly, then chief of USAF information, was to take command of the Torrejon air force base in Spain and the press corps were to give him a farewell party. Thus our first full dress social engagement consisted of marching around a vast hall filled with 500 people, preceded by a contingent of the multi-ethnic kilted USAF pipers band playing their bagpipes fortissimo, between General and Mrs Le Bailly, in front, and his son Captain (US army) and his wife behind. Press coverage next morning failed to commend the new British naval attaché to the reigning chief of naval operations on whom I was due to pay my first call .

My prime target, I had been briefed, was Admiral Rickover the 'father' of nuclear powered submarines, whose continued help in the Polaris project we so much appreciated but whose occasional tantrums were apt to cut off advice at crucial moments. Though there was no personal animosity against my predecessor, for Rickover's gall was reserved for the UK end of the Polaris affair, he had severed relations with the British embassy including my office. I had been his aide, years before, during the launching of *HM S/M Dreadnought* and, like Rickover, I was an engineer. Could I break the apparent log jam? My request for an audience was ignored, so the ambassador wrote personally, inviting Rickover to the Queen's Birthday Party (to which he had always been formally asked but had neither replied nor appeared). Again there was no answer. However, although even Maggie Phillips with her Washington expertise failed to realise it, Rickover was moving our way. One morning she received a telephone call from a young USN ensign asking if he and his friend could be placed on the embassy social list as they wished to meet some British people. That list was confined to higher ranking contacts, but with two rather bored teenage daughters at home I was anxious to produce some young eligibles. The ensigns had implied to Maggie that they belonged to some high security organisation so they seemed likely to be reliable and might fit the bill. Thus, for two or three weeks (and indeed for many months after) two delightful young men, Bob Kroll and Gerry Doyle, were frequent visitors to our house. Soon afterwards I received a summons from a genial Rickover and, in his outer office, spotted these two grinning from ear to ear and in no way embarrassed. So Rickover came to the Queen's Garden Party, his relations with the Polaris project improved slightly and we remained friends and occasional correspondents until his death.

There were several RN pilots and observers instructing at the US navy fighter station at Miramar (of *Top Gun* fame). With Britain then buying Phantoms in quantity an early visit to this group was essential. In turn they insisted that their admiral should be the first of that rank to fly in a Phantom at mach 2 and an evening in their large rented house somehow induced me to accept their madcap scheme. Not until we had taken off did Lieutenant Dick Lord RN reveal that this particular mark of Phantom had to be taken to a great height and then dived to achieve the necessary speed. Although there was an admiral suffering from shock in the rear cockpit, they gave me my wings and a mach 2 lapel badge that night in El Ponderosa, coupled with much liquid nerve restorer.

Our British naval aviators impressed a US navy greatly addicted to air power. They received citations for airmanship and a presidential citation also. At Patuxent River, the USN test pilots' school, one of our pilots received the US Navy League award for best test pilot of the year. Indeed the whole Phantom development programme owed much of its great success to the bravery of one British naval test pilot whose coolness during an early test flight enabled the reasons for a sudden temporary engine failure to be diagnosed and subsequently corrected. Speechifying was a frequent chore and I seem to have given almost one a month in my first two years. But just as the USN admires our naval aviators, this admiration is reciprocated in full. The Royal Navy has presented a number of trophies for annual competition by various types of US naval air squadrons, and one of the duties of the attaché is to present these. After the ceremony there is always tea or coffee with the enlisted men and their wives then, usually by 1030 am, officers and their guests are stuck into fierce American martinis. After one such prizegiving, still in full regalia including sword, and my escorts full to their eyebrows, we raced to the airport where my sword was forcefully and not too politely removed by the sky marshal. Some days later William Hickey proclaimed, *British admiral surrenders his sword.* The most touching ceremony was when I was asked to award commissions into the US Naval Reserve, in front of their parents and friends, to a class of young aviators. This, I was told, was an unique event and I have a photo of them all on my wall. Several used to write as their training progressed and one or two came to stay as they passed through Washington DC. But then they went off to Vietnam and we heard no more.

The US naval hierarchy were infinitely kind to us and Admiral Tom Moorer and his vice chief of naval operations Admiral Clairey, aviation and submarine aces respectively of world war two and 'Eph' Holmes as SACLANT at Norfolk, Virginia never failed to give us their time whenever we asked, however little we could do in return. But on Trafalgar Night we dined them all and I was fortunate that my time coincided with the moment when Moorer and some of his contemporaries from the famous Annapolis Class of 1933 were all in or near Washington. Pam had Carrie Moorer and the other wives to dinner at 4807 and we relayed the speeches live. It was the same with the secretaries of the navy, Nitze, Ignatius, Chafee and Warner: all made themselves available when we sought their views.

The most critical address I had to give was undoubtedly when Moorer asked me to speak to 50 of his senior officers on the British concept for operating Harrier aircraft from what we then called our through-deck cruisers (to avoid mentioning the controversial word carrier).   It triggered an invitation to demonstrate the Harrier to the US navy and US marine corps which we laid on with the help of the air attaché.   The US marines now operate a considerable Harrier force.

Louis Heren of *The Times*, Jeremy Campbell of *The Evening Standard*, Ross Mark of *The Daily Express*, Henry Brandon of *The Sunday Times* and others showed us much of America outside the diplomatic and naval circles in which any attaché is apt to be engulfed.   Through Henry Brandon I met the great Dick Helms, director of central intelligence, who was to play an influential part in my life.   His English wife, Cynthia, had been one of the attractive WRNS handling boats in Plymouth harbour in the blitz. The busy British joint services mission was apt to neglect the think-tanks that abound in North America but spurred on by Alastair Buchan I got to know many of those able men who ran them.   Chet Cooper, Dave Abshire, Frank Barnett, Robert Pfaltzgraff, the Godsons, Jackie Davies, Ed Feulner and many others have continued to guide my stumbling footsteps through the years, and made me more aware of the gigantic international problems we all face.

After Martin Luther King's assassination negroes in their hundreds trekked by mule wagon from the deep south to Washington DC where, from matchwood and cardboard, they built 'Resurrection City' opposite the great memorial to Abraham Lincoln.   In 1968 May was wet and the conditions under which they existed created a stench that spread as far as the White House.   But they stayed on in a rain-sodden, sullen protest.

Soon after, Washington exploded.   During the forenoon in the Old Navy Building I began to sense trouble.   Traffic volume seemed greater, radios were tuned in to excited commentaries. Gradually the building's 10,000 occupants vanished and rioting was reported close to.   It was clear that soon only the British navy staff would be left, so we shut up shop, piled our girls into the old Daimler, told the male staff to take the day off and joined an eight-lane traffic jam moving at about a mile an hour.   The radios told us, and indeed we could see the great pall of smoke, that the centre of Washington was on fire and had been abandoned.   Looting was reported as widespread.   So we dropped the girls at their various homes, warning them to stay indoors until we rang and to keep in touch with me or my chief staff officer Captain (later Vice Admiral Sir James) Jungius.

At home, when I finally won through, I found Pam to be worried not so much by the radio reports, for we were some way from the centre of town, but because a helpful and concerned neighbour had called round to say he was keeping a shotgun by the door, *in case those nigras get out here.* With no shot guns in the house she had wisely extracted the most formidable weapon she could find, my niblick.

Things are never done by halves in the States. That evening a curfew was proclaimed and more than 12,000 troops took over the capital. Our house was a few hundred yards into Maryland, so reaching the embassy for meetings was tricky. There were road blocks on Massachusetts Avenue, each manned by enthusiastic doughboys who might or might not have a bullet up the spout of their rifles: as all petrol stations were closed and guarded car journeys had to be carefully gauged. Although rioting in Washington was the worst (with 61 clothing stores, 57 liquor stores, 53 supermarkets and 19 drug stores looted and burned) the capital was not unique. Across the States, 125 cities erupted and nearly 70,000 troops were deployed. The scale of violence was unprecedented, except for a country verging on revolution and within a few days we were expecting two of our latest ships, *Fife* and *Glamorgan* to dock in the very centre of the city. The ambassador had put aside time to visit and entertain some of both ship's companies. The US chief of naval operations followed, eventually, by 2000 Pentagon officers were to visit the ships. Vice President Hubert Humphrey, claiming Welsh descent, insisted on joining the Washington St David's society for a morning of Welsh hymn singing in *Glamorgan*. Sufficient invitations had come from Washington's citizenry to ensure that every crew member could be entertained privately. The commandant of the naval district was to host a large party in his historic home, one of the few still standing after Rear Admiral Cockburn's troops had burned the White House and most of the city just over 150 or so years earlier on August 24, 1814. We had arranged with Bobbie Kennedy that the crippled children in a home to which he gave much time would have a party such as only the Royal Navy can provide. Should we play safe and cancel the visit ? I took a chance, the ships arrived and the programme went ahead.

Hubert Humphrey, surrounded by sinister men in dark glasses,

Greatly encouraged he asked us to send a signal to Prince Charles saying he was enjoying himself on Welsh soil (*HMS Glamorgan*) and he received a quick and warm reply. My extrovert USAF 'cousin', General Ben Le Bailly, in Washington for a few days from Torrejon, appeared in uniform and without warning accompanied by Tom McKnew, chairman of *The National Geographic Magazine*.

Hey, Louis, he hailed me from the dockside, *we've come to see over your ship and drink some rum with the Queen's Navee,* and they marched on board into the middle of a rather formal function. Observing the horrified looks of the quarterdeck staff and knowing that most of the officers were already showing VIPs over the ships, I led them to the chief petty officers' mess, most of whom had been Pam's guests the day before, and out came the bottles of (illicit) rum. Neither of them actually saw round the ship - but when I returned an hour later my cousin was leading the mess in sea shanties (as interpreted by the US Air Force). I felt it best for them to decline further hospitality and guided them gently down the for'd gangway to their car.

I have never been more proud of the Royal Navy in peacetime than I was by the end of those five days. Thousands, from every ethnic background, came on board; hundreds of British sailors went ashore and there was not a single untoward incident despite the still prevailing tenseness in a city so recently on fire. The black

• *Mayor Walter Washington inspecting HMS Fife*

the still prevailing tenseness in a city so recently on fire. The black mayor, Walter Washington, put his finger on the visit's success when he said over lunch, later, *before your ships came in I had a riot-torn city, now it seems an oasis of peace.*

Then Bobby Kennedy was assassinated in Los Angeles on June 5 1968 and all the tension returned. His body was flown to New York on the night of June 6 and next day more than 100,000 mourners paid their last respects. A funeral mass was held on June 8 and then the coffin was taken by train due to arrive at Washington at five that evening but which did not reach the Capital until well after nine o'clock. The procession stopped at the Justice Department where Bobby had worked as attorney-general and then moved on to the Arlington national cemetery where the flame on Jack Kennedy's grave flickered in the night, via the Lincoln Memorial and 'Resurrection City'. Here the negroes of the Poor People's Campaign pressed forward, some of them kneeling in the road, some of them in tears, quietly singing their old spirituals.

Robert Kennedy's murder, coming so soon after that of Martin Luther King, was a shattering blow to the Democratic party, the blacks, the hispanics, the under privileged and particularly the young. Political violence has for long been part of American history but with Bobby's death coming on top of that of his brother, of Medgar Evers, Rockwell and King there was talk of conspiracy and urban guerrilla warfare. There was a feeling of where will it all end? But end it did, surprisingly quickly. There was an election ahead and so everyone returned to the hustings and the Democrats even began to believe someone else could be found to unite the anti-war faction. There was talk of a draft for Edward Kennedy. But he was not of the calibre of his brothers; and finally Nixon, the Republican got home and Humphrey, the Democratic candidate despite his Welsh hymns on board *Glamorgan,* conceded defeat.

That summer Admiral Sir Michael Le Fanu (First Sea Lord-designate) and his chair-bound wife, Prue, came to stay with us. Le Fanu and I entertained the neighbourhood by showing my Royal Marine driver and a 'borrowed' US Marine, how to carry her up and down the steep steps outside our house, a technique into which I had been introduced when I was Michael's naval assistant. Admiral Moorer gave a splendid lunch in the Pentagon to which, almost uniquely, Admiral Rickover turned up. Currently he was more than usually disliked by the US naval hierarchy for telling a congressional committee, when asked his views on the 'Honor Code' at the Naval Academy, *that it taught the young men to lie to their seniors so that, later in life, they could mislead Congress.* Like most people, though, Rickover succumbed to the Le Fanu magic.

On his last afternoon Le Fanu asked me to walk with him, unheard of in Washington, but I knew where we might be reasonably safe from traffic and muggers. Rumours had reached me that I was to be the next controller of the navy, responsible for all matériel matters a post, like that of naval attaché Washington, never before held by an engineer. But my antennae told me otherwise. There were four good reasons. The General List, which had brought engineers into a more influential position in naval life, was only ten years old. It had taken 30 years after the Admiralty announced that (E) specialists would be considered as dockyard admiral superintendents for that event to be consummated. Vice Admiral Sir George Raper, a brilliant (E) specialist, rather than a naval constructor, had recently been appointed director general, ships, virtually the controller's deputy. We were close friends of long standing, but it would not be considered right to have two (E) officers in positions of such power. I had put forward views on the management of ship design which were not acceptable to many of the Royal Corps of Naval Constructors. Lastly there was a seaman contemporary who was clearly in the running and who in fact took over the post. Michael confirmed that I would not serve on his board as controller, but was relieved, I think, to hear that I had long since discarded that possibility. When I next visited London Michael, by then First Sea Lord, asked me to join a small birthday lunch he was giving Lord Fraser of North Cape. The latter had been kind to me in the Pacific, Michael had been his naval assistant and I his. Before lunch the naval secretary offered me the post of Flag Officer (now Port Admiral) The Nore, with a hint that if all went well there might be a vacancy at board level for me later on. The timing meant we should have little or no leave and more importantly, the financial implications were formidable. After two years' entertaining we had managed, just, on our allowances but the thought of having to entertain the worthy burghers of south-east England at our own expense, less the value of about one full measure of gin a day (the then entertainment allowance), not to speak of the strain on my wife, left me cold. So our American tour of duty was extended and we looked forward to revelling in what, I had no doubt, would be my last post before retirement.

When I arrived in the first sea lord's office both Charles Denman, his secretary, and Martin Wemyss, his naval assistant, revealed that the betting was that I would turn down the offer. *Don't think you're going to escape so easily,* was Le Fanu's comment on the way to lunch. London holds many surprises but the sight that met us at the Savoy's side entrance, where there was a lift to convey the 81-year-old admiral of the fleet up to the River Room, was unforgettable. Lieutenant Griffin RNVR had been a rather war-battered but popular messmate in *HMS Duke of York* in the Pacific. Now the Savoy general manager, dressed in a morning coat and armed with a bucket, a mop and naval squeegee, he was washing down the pavement for his old commander-in-chief.

Washington later ensured that I should come to the end of my naval career, or so I thought, with a splendid bust up. Successive devaluations had hit all service, but not civilian, allowances. While we attachés could trim our entertainment to whatever allowances were provided, this was impossible for more junior officers. An advance of pay to purchase a car had to be repaid to the Admiralty and necessarily they were all in debt for a loan, negotiated through a bank, to purchase furniture for their houses from their predecessors. These scurvy, badly thought out and sudden cuts had an intolerable impact on these young officers, their wives and families. By then I was the longest serving attaché and though the others agreed with my views and lent their not inconsiderable weight, their careers had a future; mine I thought was ending. There followed a fractious exchange of signals which Sir Arthur Drew, that great civil servant, told me later he regarded as the most impertinent he had seen in a long career. Anyway we won by rather unfair means. Dr David Owen, then minister for the navy, was coming with his bride of a few weeks to stay with us. We made sure that his brief had copies of all the signals and ensured he personally interviewed a number of junior officers. On his return he represented our case to the secretary of state and their allowances were fully restored.

The US navy was greatly impressed by Dr Owen, as were the several think tanks to which I took him. There his quick brain, wide vision and pertinent questions rather rocked the sophisticates who met him.

To my considerable surprise I received a letter from Le Fanu telling me of my forthcoming promotion to vice-admiral, the nature of my appointment to be revealed in due course. That I was to join the defence intelligence staff I learned from the omniscient Dick Helms, head of the CIA. He, like the ambassador who also knew of it, assumed I had already been told. Naval ways are sometimes bizarre.

After 30 months in Washington our final farewell party for a few 'specials' forever endeared me to Admiral Rickover. After presenting a beautiful gift to our youngest daughter, he and his wife mingled with the other guests. A west European naval attaché bore down on him. *When are you going to tell us about your nuclear submarines, admiral?* he asked. Knowing Rickover's views on secrecy I expected him to depart in dudgeon forthwith. Instead he looked the foreign admiral up and down, *I take my orders from God but I'm not communicating with him at the moment. When I do I'll send you a telegram.*

Even after 30 months of quasi-diplomatic practice this exchange floored me, so I hastily took his arm and introduced him to the wife of a famous British General, Sir George Lea.
Are you really a Lady, asked an irrepressible Rickover.
Yes replied Lady Lea.
Oh, I thought you were just a good-looking doll came the instant reply. Luckily Pam Lea, always attractive and beautifully dressed, also had a great sense of humour. Hastily I replenished Rickover's glass with ginger ale and left them to it.

A smooth voyage back in the *SS France* suited Pam as she is not a good sailor. It would have suited me too if I had not developed what was finally diagnosed some shivery weeks later as Florida Marsh fever. Mrs Hicks was not there to meet us, but a young lieutenant came aboard with the pilot and handed me a letter from the first sea lord. The contents, when we managed to read Michael Le Fanu's normal scribble, were greatly appreciated, particularly by Pam.
Well done ALL it read, and out tumbled a rather messy bar of chocolate.

• *The author's last days in office*

CHAPTER 15

Subterranean fields 1970-1975

> *Not in Utopia - subterranean fields, -*
> *Or some secreted island, Heaven knows where!*
> *But in the very world, which is the world*
> *Of all of us, - the place where, in the end*
> *We find our happiness, or not at all!*
> *The Prelude* William Wordsworth

ON ARRIVAL HOME I was sent for by the Chief of Defence Staff, Marshal of the RAF Lord Elworthy. In telling me of my forthcoming appointment to the defence intelligence staff, he mentioned that Admiral Sir Michael Le Fanu was to relieve him in a few months. *Your job,* he said, *will be to tell those who won't listen all the things they don't want to know. That I gather,* he continued, *is what Admiral Le Fanu requires of you; and as you have served him before I expect you know the form. From some of your signals I have seen from Washington recently,* he went on, *you should need no practice.*

Sadly though it did not quite turn out as Michael Le Fanu had arranged or I had begun to hope. Because I had no experience of intelligence work it was agreed that I should first relieve the (tri-service) director of service intelligence to get some feel for the task before moving on to relieve Lieutenant-General Sir Richard Fyfe as deputy chief of defence staff (intelligence) and then perhaps later, Air Marshal Sir Harold Maguire as director general of intelligence at the ministry of defence (DGI). The incumbent of the first post, however, had no intention of going until his retirement date, some eight months ahead. So I was given the task of rewriting the syllabus for the Joint Services Staff College (which I had never attended) to convert it from its multi-national (and therefore low security) to a national high security *hot-house for*

Whitehall warriors, where they could argue to their heart's content before entering the MOD, as Mr Healey and Lord Elworthy put it.

The first three months of 1970 were thus taken up with visits all over the world and with setting down my ideas on paper while working in the palatial office of the secretary of state for war, unoccupied since the Profumo affair. Although my rather avant-garde views seemed to meet with the approval of the Vice Chief of the Defence Staff, Air Chief Marshal Sir John Barraclough, like so many of his generation of RAF officers a great student of war, and Professor Laurence Martin (now Vice-Chancellor of Newcastle-on-Tyne University) whom I proposed as Visiting Dean, they seemed to raise the blood pressure of some of VCDS' single service colleagues, so that Barraclough felt it wiser for me not to listen to their discussions. Anyway, it was time to start my indoctrination into the intelligence service and a brave and resolute air commodore was selected to put my suggestions for a National Defence College into practical form.

Apart from getting to know the other members of the defence intelligence staff, I felt that I should tour the Middle East, an area my father had known well. Towards the end of his life he had interested himself in the prophecies derived from the great Pyramid which seemed to suggest that the final Armageddon would start in the original Garden of Eden, between the Tigris and Euphrates, where he had worked. The emergence of Israel, the problems of Egypt, Syria, Iraq, Jordan, Kuwait, Iran and the other Gulf States seemed, in 1970, also to point that way. Armed with a supply of Lomotil and Strepto-triad, I flew first to Bahrein, then Muscat and was about to fly to Salalah when Sultan Qaboos took over from his father. As it was felt undiplomatic to arrive in the middle of the coup I went to Niswa instead flying out later with some wounded after a rather vicious bomb attack.. From the Oman I moved on, earlier than planned, to the Trucial States (now the United Arab Emirates).

To fill the unexpected gap in my programme I joined a Bedouin patrol of the Trucial Oman Scouts, under a British officer, in the sandy wastes of the Empty Quarter. While being served stewed goat I learned from the BBC World Service that Admiral Sir Michael Le Fanu, on medical advice, had withdrawn from the post of chief of defence staff which he was about to assume. I had known he had not been well but I had hoped, like everyone else, that it was just overtiredness and that his recent holiday in Cyprus would have set him up. I did not much enjoy the goat; nor the remainder of my interesting tour of the region.

I saw Michael again only once. Both of us and our wives were asked to a celebratory lunch given at Sutton Place by Paul Getty for a friend of his, a US Marine brigadier whom Michael and I knew. Leukaemia is a strange disease. Michael, to whom I owed so much and now knew so well, was at the top of his normal scintillating form causing even the rather withdrawn Paul Getty to come out of his shell. A few weeks later, quite suddenly, he was dead. My wife was ill and could not come to the Abbey so I took Michael's SAS sergeant bodyguard who had looked after him so well in the last steamy difficult days in Aden, where Michael had been Commander-in-Chief.

I had known him for 40 years and twice had served him directly. Rather than retire at 55 a new career in the inter-service intelligence world seemed, with Michael as my boss, an acceptable change of scene. Now he was gone and I was about to step into a strange twilight. The Defence Intelligence Staff (DIS) was Mountbatten's last brainchild and the first truly integrated part of the ministry of defence. Under an intelligence-experienced general and air marshal, the three single service intelligence organisations had been integrated with the scientific, engineering and economic echelons of the Joint Intelligence Bureau and were learning to work together amicably.

With the blessing of Lord Elworthy and his successor, Admiral of the Fleet Sir Peter Hill-Norton (later Lord Hill-Norton and chairman of the NATO military committee), I cautiously approached the faintly hostile intelligence experts. Many, especially civilians, as they made clear to me, had long and honourable careers in intelligence stretching back several decades which was sometimes the trouble. My debut was less than encouraging. My wife and I had bought an old house in Wiltshire and rented a flat in Dolphin Square which could just accommodate us both when she came up to town. It was not until after we had moved in that we discovered the last tenant but one had been Vassall, the naval spy. In some embarrassment I confidentially reported this and quickly discovered the Whitehall capacity for 'leaks'. Within 48 hours the news was in the press. The civilian experts were as suspicious of me as I of them.

The second problem also occurred through the press. *The Times* devoted several inches suggesting that I was the prime

Royal Navy expert on the make-up and intentions of the Soviet navy. The brave and boyish editor, Charlie Douglas-Home, had long been a friend and often an ally, but the seaman naval intelligence group, disturbed at the thought of answering to an engineer, certainly did not agree and went on the defensive.

The third problem was Ireland, by 1970 already bubbling dangerously. Here, happily for me, the army and RAF, who both seemed to regard me as an innocent abroad to be educated gently, took me in hand. Besides looking after me as the troubles escalated, they taught me a great deal and , with the police, protected my family as our house was near a great air station.

Largely as a result of my own inadequacy, though it was a deeply interesting period, my five years in the DIS were the least happy in the 46 years of my service. My more able and experienced predecessors had made good headway in bringing together the three services and the engineering, scientific and economic echelons. With the help and encouragement of a great permanent secretary, Sir James Dunnett and his opposite number at the Foreign and Commonwealth office, Sir Denis (now Lord) Greenhill and the secretary to the cabinet, the late Lord Trend, it was my task to give the department a sharper cutting edge. This, it was hoped, would enable its often uniquely correct assessments to carry more weight within the MOD and Whitehall generally. To accomplish this whilst reducing numbers, 'old Spanish customs' and the high average age provoked a surge of highly charged emotion. To cool it consumed so much of my time and energy that I was frustrated at my inability to partake to the extent I believed desirable in the assessment process of the DIS politico/military/economic/scientific input of intelligence so critically important to the national product.

But there were happy times. In my first two years I was personally looked after by a succession of outstanding majors (now both brigadiers), Dick Hume, an Irish Guards officer and Dermot Blundell-Hollinshead-Blundell, a Grenadier. Both loyally guided my stumbles through the corridors of power and usually managed to forewarn me of the storms that blew around my head when my credibility was questioned. Best of all, when the situation appeared wholly black, they made me laugh. In my last two years, General Sir John Younger, a Coldstream this time, cheerfully and more effectively than I could have done took most of the administration of the new style DIS off my shoulders.

To become director general of intelligence and therefore directly responsible to the secretary of state I was asked, *in the national interest,* and much against my wishes, to become a temporary civil servant. There could only be one reply, but by leaving the navy early it was never revealed to me that my pension would be diminished; worse that my widow's also will be considerably reduced. To this there is apparently no redress.

The post of DGI brought me into contact with the intelligence community often in personal peril who seem always to be under attack by those elements of the media and politicians spewing out Soviet disinformation. In a world in which civilisation itself was under threat, most of these intensely loyal men and women were doing a most difficult job in freedom's cause about as well as it could be done.

I wrote earlier of how the threat from Soviet Russia is so often misinterpreted and how intimidation and blackmail are the Kremlin's main weapons. Recently I have realised that for every unit of energy of home-produced food we eat, Britain's 'efficient' farmers expend ten units of fossil fuel energy, much of it imported. Environmental problems apart it is a strange British doctrine indeed that views, apparently with equanimity, a Soviet submarine fleet five times the size of the German force that all but brought us to our knees in 1942.

After five years in the defence intelligence staff the then secretary of state, that staunch patriot Roy Mason and his permanent secretary, the late Sir Michael Cary, tried to talk me into staying on as director general of intelligence. But the reorganisation was complete, the DIS, I felt, had enough self confidence not to trim but *to go on telling those who wouldn't listen all the things they didn't want to know.* My deputy, a dynamic lieutenant-general, was positively itching to get into my shoes and at the other end my heart was starting to fibrillate so it seemed a good moment to invoke the break clause in my contract with the civil service. Both army and air force were good to me. The Berlin garrison and General Harrod entertained me famously for 24 hours. General Sir Harry Tuzo, the deputy SACEUR, whose hospitality I had previously enjoyed when he commanded in Northern Ireland, made me 'sing' to his full staff for a subsequent magnificent 'supper'. I was a guest at an army board dinner in Chelsea Hospital. The RAF, still repentant at damaging my ears in the preliminaries to a high level reconnaissance mission, entertained me at a cocktail party at

Strike Command: while Sir Michael Cary and Sir Thomas Brimelow from the Foreign and Commonwealth Office, the CDS FM Sir (later Lord) Carver and deputy chief of the air staff, also gave me a dinner next door to a restaurant where the metropolitan police were conducting, fairly noisily, the Spaghetti House siege. Somehow I weathered a stupendously alcoholic lunch given by the foreign and commonwealth attachés, with the Soviet naval attaché, the doyen, presiding; and only a few days before I had been enjoying roast duck in Peking. I understood my own service well enough to know that the Board of Admiralty would be unlikely to indulge in any similar light-hearted frivolity. Nor did they. However, after a gentle prod, the vice chief of naval staff sent me back to sea.

HMS Sheffield was the first major all gas-turbined operational warship and so of enormous interest to me in my long-discarded (E) specialist hat. Besides my able civilian personal assistant, John Cunningham, I took Mr (later Sir Colin) Fielding my newly joined director of scientific and technical intelligence with me. The captain asked us to talk to the wardroom and then to the chief and petty officers and on the rating's messdecks. The depth and perceptiveness of their questioning was impressive.

All this revelry impelled a worried John Cunningham to make a medical appointment for me. When I had officially left the navy three years earlier to become director general the problems of tinittus (noises in the head) and an inability to hear high notes, both results of bomb blast in *HMS Naiad*, had been recorded; now a young naval doctor put me through the same routine aural investigations and clearly expected me to depart. Hesitantly I mentioned, blood pressure (the attachés lunch in mind), asbestosis (we had all lived in a fog of asbestos dust when boiler cleaning in my younger days and several (E) specialists had died of it), fibrillation (from which rather frighteningly I seemed to be suffering).

Heavens, no sir, the young medico replied, *we don't examine old men these days . We might find someting wrong.* Thus my feeling that I had come to the end of the road was amply confirmed. It was time to say 'good bye'.

Index